WIDE WELCOME

WIDE WELCOME

HOW THE UNSETTLING PRESENCE OF NEWCOMERS CAN SAVE THE CHURCH

JESSICAH KREY DUCKWORTH

Fortress Press

Minneapolis

WIDE WELCOME

How the Unsettling Presence of Newcomers Can Save the Church

Scripture quotations are from the New Revised Standard Version Bible, copyright © 1989 by the Division of Christian Education of the National Council of the Churches of Christ in the USA. Used by permission. All rights reserved.

Cover image: *Church Interior with Pews and Open Door* © Ocean Photography/Veer.com
Cover design: Alisha Lofgren

Library of Congress Cataloging-in-Publication Data is available
Print ISBN: 978-0-8006-9939-0
E-book ISBN: 978-1-4514-2625-0

The paper used in this publication meets the minimum requirements of American National Standard for Information Sciences — Permanence of Paper for Printed Library Materials, ANSI Z329.48-1984.

Manufactured in the U.S.A.

This book was produced using PressBooks.com, and PDF rendering was done by PrinceXML.

CONTENTS

Acknowledgments

Multiple communities of practice have given shape to this book. For the teachers and colleagues of Princeton Theological Seminary who surrounded me throughout my doctoral work I give thanks. For Dr. Richard Osmer who always placed the nugget of wisdom within my reach that I might find my voice as a scholar, I am eternally grateful. Thank you to Dr. Kenda Dean and Dr. Gordon Mikoski, who, with Dr. Osmer, created and held an environment of mutual respect for one another that gave birth to my own identity as scholar and vocation as wife, mother, pastor, student, friend, and colleague. The Lilly Foundation and the practical theology department at Princeton Theological Seminary funded my primary research through the Faithful Practices Project. Through the grant I met newcomers, congregational members, catechists, and pastors willing to share the wisdom of their newcomer welcome processes. I will always treasure these conversations and visits for the hospitality and grace I received as a researcher. I am also thankful for my colleagues at Wesley Theological Seminary, Luther Seminary, and the Wabash Center who supported me as I finished this book. I could not have written these pages without the questions and contributions of students at both Wesley and Luther.

My mentor and friend, Dr. Margaret Krych, taught me how to think theologically, think practically, and care deeply about the church's teaching and learning ministries. For your deep font of wisdom I give thanks to God. My parents lent their ear and their editing skills to this project for many years. You taught me to love Jesus and the church. Both were necessary for these ideas to take shape. Thank you.

My husband Chris has persistently said, "You can do this." Who would have imagined our married life of ten years would include so many surprises and blessings—particularly our children Talitha, Cana, and Naaman. For Chris's steady and loving support of our partnership and life together under the grace of the Triune God, I give thanks. Thank you, my love, for agreeing to walk this way with me.

Soli Deo Gloria.
Easter 2013

Introduction

As a young girl growing up in Baltimore, Maryland, I would often take trips to the ocean with my family. I loved walking down the sandy shore with my siblings, picking up seashells and rocks, and tossing them back into the water. I watched the waves crest and fall, bringing in new shells and carrying others away. Between our forays into the ocean with our father, my mother, who was never too excited about the cold water, would crouch in the sand for hours, crafting a magnificent and intricate sand castle. My brothers, sister, and I would watch. At times, we would even try to help, getting into the sand with our hands and shovels and buckets. In our enthusiasm, when we would accidentally step in a tunnel and collapse it, we would try to rebuild it together.

One summer when my daughter was young, I tried to build a sand castle, and it was a complete failure. I built it too far from the water's edge, and the sand dried too quickly from the heat of the rising sun. I elicited my husband's help to bring buckets of water from the ocean, but as we raced to keep the walls up with water, other parts of the tunnel and walls would collapse. The castle became a perfect playground for my daughter's feet.

After my dreadful attempt to build a sand castle, I e-mailed my mother for advice and tips for the task. The trick to an excellent sand structure, she reminded me, is to build it close enough to the water so that, digging deep, one finds the moist sand that is the key to holding the structure together. At the same time, the structure needs to be far enough away from the water that the sand is not overly moist and that there is little chance a large wave will wash away the structure as it is still being created.

My mother would situate herself near the high-water line and douse the spot with water. Then she would begin the slow process of building a huge pile of tightly packed wet sand for the foundation. One does not begin to construct a sand castle in the hole, as I was trying to do; the building process occurs by sculpting the structure down from a larger pile of moist sand. Using her hands, the edge of a shovel, or a plastic knife from our lunch cooler, my mother would form, mold, shape, and carve the sand pile into a tower or series of walls. She would smile at our ill-fated attempts to create a tower out of dry sand in our buckets, and she would come to our aid by repacking our buckets with a mixture of wet and dry sand. She would move around the pile, reshaping, repacking, and recarving the creations of her young apprentices. I imagine now that our immature contributions often disrupted my mother's vision for the castle of the day.

Our family's creation usually piqued the interest of families gathered around us, too. More often than not, complete strangers would pick up a shovel and begin to help. Just as the sea was in constant motion a few feet from our toes, so too my mother's creative vision ebbed and flowed with her children's attempts and failures and the intrusions of those around us. At the end of the morning, we would step back and marvel at our creation.

Still, we knew that as the day wore on, nothing would protect our family's creation. Inevitably with the tide change, we would have to shift our towels and blankets away from the rising water and watch our castle fall to the enfolding waves. Sand is a temporary medium. No matter how much work it took or whether we liked it or not, the sea would take back the shore. Building sand castles is a pretty foolish task. When one sand castle enthusiast was asked why she spends so much time building something that is just going to be washed away by the tide, she said, "Sandcastles are very much like life; the joy comes from the process of living and building and not in the act of completion."[1] As we left the beach after our visits, all we took away was the memory of our shared task—building our structure of sand—and the joy that comes from the process of living and building, not in the act of completion.

The process of building a sand castle only to watch it fall again is an apt metaphor for a church of the cross (the *ecclesia crucis*). The *ecclesia crucis* is sustained by the Holy Spirit, resisting desires for established permanence and insisting that, for the church to be church, it must include newcomers in the practices of discipleship. The *ecclesia crucis* does not need to dread the falling sand castle because joy comes from the fluidity and movement of newcomers and established members being and becoming disciples of Jesus Christ alongside one another. Mainline Protestant congregations in North America often desire permanence with an established membership as the solid foundation. With this premise, newcomers are not necessary. The *ecclesia crucis* beckons irresistibly to be sculpted and carved, reshaped and repacked by young and old, newcomer and established member together.

WELCOMING NEWCOMERS

In the following chapters, I will examine how congregations in the Evangelical Lutheran Church in America welcome newcomers. I prefer the word *newcomer* to *unchurched, unbaptized, visitor,* or *potential new member* because it does not qualify the person's presence with anything other than the amount of time spent in relation to the congregation. I will use *newcomer* broadly to refer to any of three categories of persons who are initiating a process of exploring and joining a congregation: unbaptized adults, active Christians moving to a new congregation, and previously inactive baptized Christians. I will not explore welcoming newcomers from the perspectives of evangelism, mission, or hospitality—all of which are the subjects of significant bodies of literature in their own right. Rather, I am examining this ministry of welcoming newcomers as an educator who recognizes that newcomers must learn how to live as disciples.[2] Discipleship is learned through participation in congregational practices such as Bible study, prayer, worship, care for one another, service toward neighbor, and many others. Newcomers gain knowledge and skill only as they participate in congregational practices over time, together with established members. Established members are Christians counted on membership rolls, and they include active (worshipping) participants, less regular (worshipping) participants, and inactive members who do not participate.

To welcome newcomers, I propose a catechesis of the cross, or a *cruciform catechesis*, a type of learning that arises from newcomers and established members participating together in Christian discipleship practices. *Catechesis* is an old word for learning and means to "sound or echo in the ear."[3] I appreciate this old word because it reminds us that Christian discipleship practices have a relationship with the past. The stories about these practices arise out of Jesus' own practice, the witness of the first followers of Jesus, and the church's commitment to figuring out what faithfulness looks like in every era. To learn to be a disciple is to learn these practices and their stories.

Discipleship is not innate; we are not born disciples of Jesus Christ. Discipleship is experienced and learned; we become disciples of Jesus Christ. Thus, attention to learning or catechesis is necessary within the church. Discipleship and faith are interrelated, mutually informing one another. Discipleship and faith are also distinct. Discipleship is learning through participation in Christian practices, gaining knowledge and skill to sustain a Christian identity. To be clear, faith is not learned. Faith cannot be reduced to knowledge or skill. Faith is a gift of the Holy Spirit. Faith sustains and enables the life of disciples within and beyond the *ecclesia crucis*. In this book, I will reference discipleship more often than faith because I am attending specifically to those practices of Christianity that must be learned because they are not innate. Yet I will be careful not to draw the distinction too far, because discipleship and faith*fulness* (the response of faith) are synonyms.

I have added *cruciform* as a modifier of *catechesis* to situate participation in Christian discipleship practices at the foot of the cross. In catechesis at the foot of the cross, certainty loosens its grip, knowing breaks down, and truth and reality are turned upside down. On the cross, where God is fully absent, God is simultaneously fully present. In the crucified God, God is fully alive. Only faith, as a gift of the Spirit, can hold this paradox. Only *as* disciples can we learn what it means to *be* disciples of the cross. Another way to say this is that, at the foot of the cross, everything appears under its opposite, even the church. For the Christian church to be church, newcomers, who may or may not know what it means to be a disciple or who may or may not have received the gift of faith, must be present.

Newcomers call the church to its task of "making disciples." Making disciples is the life-sustaining, life-saving work that makes up the church's identity. The church does not seek permanence with established membership as the solid foundation, but fluidity and movement of newcomers and established members together. Thus, the life of the church depends upon a newcomer's presence within the body of Christ. Newcomers may be an unsettling presence, but they are saving the church.

A Cruciform Catechesis

A cruciform catechesis is an ecclesiological discipleship-making process that engages the conditions and reality of the world today, insisting that newcomers are indispensable participants of the *ecclesia crucis*. A newcomer's presence within a congregation reminds the congregation that there are people who do not yet belong. This reminder is most unsettling because the majority of established members experience their congregation as a promising context where they are nurtured in faith, hope, and love. Established members assume that newcomers experience this promise as naturally as they do.

When the Holy Spirit gathers people together, promises are declared. Jesus said, "Where two or three are gathered, I am there among them."[4] Established members know this promise. In the hearing of scripture and proclamation of the gospel, faith awakens. Every baptism rehearses the covenantal declaration, "You have been sealed by the Holy Spirit, and marked with the cross of Christ forever."[5] Hope is extended at every fellowship meal in which a sense of blessedness hovers lightly and invisibly around the room. From confession to fellowship, Bible study to finance committee, Sunday school to soup kitchen, the confirmation of God's promise grounds all of ministry—implicitly and explicitly—in love. God's determination to claim this world in the cross is heard again and again in God's covenant with the people of Israel, "I will be your God, and you will be *my* people."[6] The established members of a Christian congregation hear the promise of divine kinship alongside the people of Israel, "You are my people," and claim their identity too as a people belonging to God.

When a newcomer enters the congregation, the promising context becomes unsettled. Just who are "*my* people"? The presence of the newcomer reveals a question underlying the promise, and this question unsettles the established members already convinced of who and whose they are. Newcomers sit in the pew perhaps, but they are not yet committed to be "*my* people," and more, the congregation is not yet committed to welcoming them as "my people." The newcomer's question, "Who are *my* people?" reverberates within the life of the people under the cross, creating an unsettling tension between question and promise—a setting for a cruciform catechesis.[7]

A cruciform catechesis holds on to both the newcomer's questioning presence and the congregation's promising context. Some congregations will think they are welcoming yet fail to entertain or engage the newcomer's questioning presence. The difference is in the kind of questioning presence that is entertained. Does the congregation ask, "Who is this person?" without addressing the newcomer directly? It is natural for congregations to seek to reduce the tension between promise and question, for it is much easier to be a people hearing the promise and relishing God's promises "for us." Thus, there is a rush on the part of established church members and leaders to bring newcomers quickly into membership with a three-week class designed to tell them what they need to know. This rush satisfies the desire to get back to a comfortable equilibrium of the membership organization, where the promise of the gospel is proclaimed in comfort and familiarity. The side effect is that the promise extended to the newcomer is reduced to a general proclamation, "Everyone is welcome here; it doesn't matter who you are." Established members never have to ask the newcomer directly, "Who are you?" Tension disappears when newcomers and their questions are ignored.

This tension between promise and question exists only when newcomer questions are engaged within the church. Tension is created when the congregation asks the newcomer, "Who are you?" and then listens deeply to the response. I invite congregations to welcome newcomers and their unsettling questions as a means of grace. As gifts of the Holy Spirit, the means of grace create and sustain faith through an encounter with the living Word of God, Jesus Christ. The means of grace are the places where Jesus promises to show up—through the word of God, through the sacraments, and in the Christian community. Through the Spirit's power, the church is called to steward these means. Established members come to trust these means and even, perhaps, take them for granted. If, however, the *ecclesia crucis* sees and encounters God where we least likely expect God to show up, then newcomers and their questions are a means of cruciform grace. Newcomers are angels unawares.[8] Jesus taught the disciples to expect and provide hospitality for unexpected guests. Newcomers are the people we least expect to bear the image of Jesus. The *ecclesia crucis* anticipates and prepares for those who come questioning the promise, expecting them to be promise bearers.[9] To face the questioned promise and remain in the tension, rather than seek to resolve it quickly, is the posture of welcome that makes space for newcomers and established members together to interrogate the question "Who are *my* people?"

And more, a cruciform catechesis is the learning that breaks open the possibility for established members to engage the question implicit within themselves. Since God's promises sometimes appear elusive, it is also easy for established members in congregations to spend their Sunday morning trying to pin down the promises for themselves. Protecting these promises would be as successful as my family's desire to protect our sand castle from the encroaching waves. Rather than protecting God's promises for ourselves or protecting "our" church castles from the waves of newcomer questions, I invite congregations to encourage newcomers in asking the questions that established members also ask. When established members engage the questions alongside newcomers, all are encouraged to articulate the promise of divine kinship and figure out together what faithfulness and belonging look like. Newcomer questions are the waves that bear the moisture and new sand, allowing for the ongoing re-creation of the church.

The setting for a cruciform catechesis is anywhere newcomers and established members participate together in Christian discipleship practices. A Bible study, prayer group, a service opportunity, and worship are all possible settings. The aim of a cruciform catechesis is a church marked by the Pauline virtues of faith, hope, and love.[10]

For Douglas John Hall, the Christian church as a people under the cross confesses faith, not sight; hope, not optimism; and love, not power.[11] This promise-filled confession of faith, hope, and love is never reconciled in a satisfying way but is filled with the tension of real life-saturated questions. Sight, optimism, and power are marks of a Christian church reducing tension and seeking triumphalism, a description of reality that is comprehensive, nonparadoxical, and entirely transcendent. Triumphalistic attitudes equate divinity with dominance, power, and victory.

Biblical faith confesses a different God. This God is, as Martin Luther would write, *Deus absconditus–Deus revelatus,* God whose self-revelation is also hidden: "For the work of God must be hidden and never understood, even when it happens. But it is never hidden in any other way than under that which appears contrary to our conceptions and ideas."[12] The church of the cross speaks of a God who is revealed in the place that reason and experience would be least likely to look: in human form in the manger and on the cross. This is a God who is compassionate—one who is "suffering-with," an incarnate God, a God in time, a God turned toward the world in love in Jesus Christ. Thus, the marks of the church of the cross are faith, hope, and love.[13]

FAITH, HOPE, AND LOVE

Faith, for Hall, is not sight or certitude but is rather "being conscious of its own incompleteness."[14] Faith is thus a category of relationship happening or occurring between the Triune God and humanity.[15] Recognizing faith as neither assent nor certitude, Hall dismisses any notion that faith happens abstractly or objectively. Faith is a gift, an experience of God's promising presence as divine within the reality of the human condition. This experience of God as divine and human cultivates trust among humans, not through compulsion, but through a relationship in which Jesus Christ in the fullness of humanity seeks joy *and* sorrow, gladness *and* grief. Faith as a category of relationship and trust is not complete without an "other"; we cannot have faith without others.

Relationships are not static but fluid and dynamic, involving deep faith and honest doubt: "One could say, God expects us to doubt; because without doubt our belief in God becomes just as routine and artificial as happens in human relationships that have lost their vitality. So don't let anyone tell you, that if you have any doubt in you, you don't believe in God, or that Christian faith has no room for unfaith. The most poignant—and accurate—prayer of the Christian is always rather like the statement of a man to Jesus in the newer Testament: 'Lord, I believe, help my unbelief' (Mark 9:24)."[16] Faithful living is also doubt-filled living, and thus it is always seeking understanding through an experience of meaning in relationship with God or with humanity.

Congregations practice faith as they confess their incompleteness without the newcomer in their midst. Eagerly anticipating the questions that will arise out of the newcomer's experiences of the human condition and the holy, congregations are called to be in relationship with an "other." Faithful, doubt-filled living is the ability to ask questions, "neither threatened by nor scornful of faiths of others; on the contrary, unlike the religiously sure-of-themselves, it is ready to listen to all seekers after God and Truth."[17] Faithful, doubt-filled living within congregations welcomes newcomer questions because the tension between promise and question is lived and not reduced.

Hall intimates that to hope is to repent of our triumphalistic ideologies of what the future will be and instead to live within the present. Hope is not pious optimism that produces a benign "peace of mind."[18] Being honest about the entropic force of death and the despair and suffering present in our lives and in the world, congregations live in the hope of the resurrection by looking toward the future with full regard for the world in which they are situated. "Hope that is fashioned 'beneath the cross of Jesus' will even, despite itself, be driven to greater and greater honesty about the data of despair, the realities that make for hopelessness."[19] However, to take a deep look at the suffering in the world is possible only with the courage given by God's grace. Courage comes from the promises contained within the means of grace (word, sacrament, and the Christian community). To confess hope for the future is to let the reality of the present and the past speak for itself,[20] and from the reality of the present and past imagine the future.

Congregations practice hope by daily dying and rising with the continuity and displacement, reproduction and transformation that inherently take place in incarnate, human organizations. In the honest confession of entropy, hope becomes tangible in those newcomers who will come and "be-come" members of the congregation. In questioning the promise, newcomers are the presence of the world within the congregation. Simultaneously, newcomers are the future of the congregation and thus announce with their presence the promise of new life given to the church. The congregational imagination of who the church might become is shaped through its encounters with newcomers in the present: "The bearing or stance appropriate to the church is not that of a community that has arrived but of one that is under way (*communio viatorum*)—that is, a community of hope."[21]

What is love? In the same way that faith is not sight but doubt and hope is not optimism but honesty about despair and hopelessness, love is not power or being powerful, but weakness and being weak. A confession of hope honest about suffering and pain engenders empathy and identification with the suffering that courageously calls upon *sola fides* (faith alone) to bear witness to the one who promises to be in relationship with us yet appears in places and people where we least expect to see the Holy Triune presence. Love is doubt-filled, courageous living not for one's self but for the sake of one's neighbor. God, who we expect to be powerful and mighty, shows us love in a manger and on a cross. This love is a suffering love identified by the poor, the sick, and the dying.

Congregations practice love through an orientation to the cross upon which God's *agape* (suffering love) is revealed. Here at the foot of the incarnate presence of the Crucified, whose spirit cried out in abandonment, the human spirit also cries, "Why?" Love becomes tangible as newcomers appear at the threshold of congregations weary, broken, and worn, searching for meaning, purpose, identity, and new life. Love is the compulsion to welcome these strangers, eager to hear their questions and announcing God's promises for them and not only for ourselves. This love transforms the congregation's orientation toward God and to the world. Hall defines the outcome of faith as the grace-given courage to engage the world.[22] The marks come full circle. Love compels this faith. "Faith in the crucified one means courage to love the world and seek one's place in it despite the world's indifference and one's own yearning for security and calm. Faith is a journey toward the world."[23]

ECCLESIA CRUCIS: A COURAGEOUS PEOPLE UNDER THE CROSS

To be a Christian church is to practice being a people under the cross. Like building sand castles, this task seems on its face pretty foolish. To be a Christian church is for the people under the cross to practice a confession of faith, hope, and love, welcoming newcomers into discipleship practices where faith meets doubt, hope meets despair, and love meets the suffering world. Hall calls the church of the cross an *ecclesia crucis*, which forms members for life in *and* beyond the local congregation:[24] "The whole purpose of this theology of the cross is to engender a movement—a people—that exists in the world under the sign of the cross of Jesus Christ: a movement and people called into being by his Spirit and being conformed to his person and furthering his work."[25] This movement, this people, is a church of the cross that embodies "the way of Jesus Christ" in its baptismal living, dying, and rising. This movement does not come from the courage of individuals, or even the courage of people, but rather from the movement of God toward the world in Jesus Christ: "The movement of the divine toward the world becomes now the necessity (the 'must') under which all of us live who through the divine Spirit have found in the crucified and risen one new life and a new beginning."[26] God's movement into the world compels the movement of all Christians into the world as disciples. The *ecclesia crucis* exists not to live but to die in being sent and scattered, propelled out into the world. This is paradoxical. This is foolishness. A sand castle paradigm of church makes explicit that by pretending to be established or by trying to be permanent, churches will ultimately dry out and crack under the heat of the sun, because this posture is antithetical to the way of the cross.

Frankly, the definition of the *ecclesia crucis* presented in this introduction does not have the look or feel of a church as many perceive church to be. Whether within a tall-steepled church, a rural country church, a Gothic cathedral, or the sprawling suburban church campus, congregational life today for many Christians is much more an experience of organizational membership than an experience of being a people gathered under the cross. Eagerly reflecting business or economic models that reward being greater, bigger, stronger, faster, and progressive, congregations actively avoid and deny death. For in the pyramid that is the committee structure of many congregations, eyes look upward to see a congregational hierarchy, established norms, and static roles for members to fulfill. With pews and mortgages, committee structures and membership classes that are akin to orientation sessions complete with slick marketing materials that make assimilation into programmatic structures seem easy, the church has become "professional," hoping that being professional will reinforce its established position within the public sphere—an establishment that has been waning in recent years.

Sand castles are not established or permanent structures, although they do have temporary form. So, too, the Christian church is given form by the means of grace: word, sacrament, and the mutual conversation and consolation among brothers and sisters.[27] Church happens in situated moments when the means of grace are present. These central practices form the church—hearing and proclaiming the word, washing in the waters of baptism and daily affirmation of that new birth, eating and drinking for the forgiveness of sins, worshipping, praying, and gathering together to console and to encourage. This helpful Lutheran definition of church as the gathering of sisters and brothers where the word is proclaimed and the sacraments are rightly administered can be understood as a very fluid and flexible definition of church, but it can also be a very insular way of defining the form of the church.[28]

In an effort to preserve the church and erect permanent structures to house the means of grace, the church turns inward, in what Martin Luther has called the typical condition of humanity, *incurvatus in se* (curved in upon oneself). To be fluid and flexible, these central practices need not be established or preserved but turned outward as the means of grace for the world. Thus, the church is rightly church *when newcomers are present.* It is the newcomers who embody the presence of the world in their implicit question, "Who are *my people?*" Then the discipleship practices of the church are given a new orientation as newcomers ask their questions alongside established members.

Newcomers step over the threshold of the mainline North American congregation for a variety of reasons. Newcomers may or may not know what to expect of the church, its programs, its culture, and its expectations. Newcomers may or may not have any sense of what will be expected of them in terms of contributing to the congregational life, tithing, volunteering, or practices related to prayer, Bible study, and Christian fellowship. But it usually does not matter what expectations or intuitions newcomers bring to a congregation, because what newcomers encounter is a comfortable, closed gathering in which their presence is not necessary needed. Newcomers are offered the static welcome of an organization seeking to be professional with an aim to assimilate the newcomer into the structure of the church. This static welcome is often found in new-member classes, pastor classes, fellowship opportunities, and rites of welcome in public worship. The aim of this welcome is often to talk about the church and its structures and the congregation's programs by presenting an array of private or public opportunities for future newcomer participation.

I will suggest that welcoming newcomers involves facilitating participation in the central practices of discipleship, alongside established membership of the congregation in the present, not the future. This is not "talking about" discipleship practices but actually doing practices of discipleship. No one possesses the action or the meaning that arises from the interaction of the gathering. These practices are personal, announcing a promise, and at the same time turn the self toward others, listening for a question from within the congregation and beyond. A cruciform catechesis of the *ecclesia crucis* is where congregations live in the tension between question and promise, practicing a confession of faith, hope, and love through the means of grace by welcoming newcomers into practices where faith meets doubt, hope meets despair, and love meets the suffering world.

Welcoming newcomers involves listening deeply to the raw data of human experience that arise out of their desire for belonging and facilitating their participation in practices of discipleship. Facilitating participation and creating a space for deep inquiry move discipleship practices toward the congregation's periphery, where newcomers dwell, if not beyond the gathering of the congregation altogether. In this very process of welcoming newcomers, God saves the church, moving the church into relationship with the world. This is a church that lives for the joy of building sand castles. This is a pretty foolish way of being church and a way that we have perhaps forgotten. We have forgotten how to begin.

Notes

1. Dennis Randall, "Stupendous Sandcastles: An Imagination Station Activity," *Family Education* (Pearson Education), http://fun.familyeducation.com/summer/outdoor-games/35066.html.

2. Unlike a habit, which is usually located in the individual, practices are inherently social and shared. Practices are not instinctual. A practice is a shared history of learning.

3. Catechesis and the family of words that surround this term, including catechetics, catechisms, and the catechumenate, have a long history within the field of Christian education. I recognize that catechesis is a foreign term within some congregations and for others might be a stumbling block. I believe catechesis is a powerful term. Recognizing that this echoing catechesis occurs within the life of a people living under the cross, I will explore the cruciform nature of catechesis as the tension between question and promise.

4. Matt. 18:20.

5. Evangelical Lutheran Church in America, *Evangelical Lutheran Worship* (Minneapolis: Augsburg Fortress, 2006), 231.

6. Douglas John Hall correlates the covenantal promise with the cross of Golgotha's claim upon this world. See Douglas John Hall, "The Theology of the Cross: A Usable Past," Evangelical Lutheran Church in America, http://www.elca.org/~/media/Files/Growing in Faith/Vocation/Word and Service Ministry/TheTheologyoftheCross_pdf.ashx.

7. Systematic theologian Paul Tillich describes the method of correlation as making "an analysis of the human situation out of which the existential questions arise, and [demonstrating] that the symbols used in the Christian message are answers to these questions." Paul Tillich, *Systematic Theology* (Chicago: University of Chicago Press, 1951), 1:62. The tension I speak of between question and promise is more complex than a simple correlation between the existential questions of the situation and the answer drawn from the symbols found in the gospel, if only because that correlation is just too calm and dispassionate in its less-than-thick description of human life in its plurality. See Tillich, *Systematic Theology*, 1:13–16. Douglas John Hall acknowledges, "For Tillich . . . the thing that prevents the theological answer from assuming the status of the absolute is the human question, which is never silenced, and the situation, which keeps changing." Douglas John Hall, *The Cross in Our Context: Jesus and the Suffering World* (Minneapolis: Fortress Press, 2003), 45. There is room for this "theory" to take on the particulars of everyday life, and I, like Hall, would like to push the correlation toward the realm of thick description. Hall asks, "What if the highly specific realities of [Tillich's] situation had been permitted to make their way as it were, more geographically and explicitly into the pages of his three-volume system of theology? It is one thing to speak theoretically about the correlation of situation and message, question and answer; it is something else to bring into proximity to one another the traditions of the faith and the existing events, conflicts, and attitudes of one's world." Hall, *Thinking the Faith: Christian Theology in a North American Context* (Minneapolis: Fortress Press, 1991), 1:360. The question embodied in the newcomer cannot be denied its complexity, and resists a simple theological answer. I refrain from using the word *answer*, preferring to describe the gospel as "promise."

8. Heb. 13:2 (KJV).

9. "Truly I tell you, just as you did it to one of the least of these who are members of my family, you did it to me" (Matt. 25:40). For when you welcomed strangers, the church welcomes Christ. "Welcome one another, therefore, just as Christ has welcomed you, for the glory of God" (Rom. 15:7).

10. The Pauline virtues of 1 Cor. 13:13 and 1 Thess. 1:3.

11. Douglas John Hall, *Why Christian?* (Minneapolis: Augsburg Fortress, 1998), 88–116.

12. Martin Luther, *Lectures on Romans, Glosses and Scholia,* vol. 25, *Luther's Works,* ed. Jaroslav Pelikan and Helmut T. Lehmann, trans. Jacob A. Preus (St. Louis: Concordia, 1972), 366.

13. I am using the phrase "marks of the church" differently than is typical for Lutherans. Martin Luther often wrote of seven marks of the church: word, sacrament (baptism and Holy Communion), forgiveness, ordination, prayer, and "the holy possession of the cross." Gordon W. Lathrop and Timothy J. Wengert, *Christian Assembly: Marks of the Church in a Pluralistic Age* (Minneapolis: Fortress Press, 2004). I use these marks in the same spirit of flexibility as Wengert and Lathrop observed: "In the writing of Luther and Melanchthon, the list of the church marks varied, with one of the most complete lists coming in Luther's tract on the church in 1539. Different situations . . . or . . . different biblical texts gave rise to different lists. However, all invariably went back to the word and the sacraments (visible words and their effects on the Christian community's confession of faith and love)" (83–84).

14. Douglas John Hall, "Theology of the Cross: Challenge and Opportunity for the Post-Christendom Church," in *Cross Examinations: Readings on the Meaning of the Cross Today,* ed. Marit Trelstad (Minneapolis: Fortress Press, 2006), 255.

15. Hall, *Why Christian?,* 91.

16. Ibid., 93.

17. Hall, "Theology of the Cross," 255.

18. Ibid., 256.

19. Ibid., 257.

20. I appreciate this phrase found in the philosophical work of Martha C. Nussbaum, *Sex and Social Justice* (New York: Oxford University Press, 1999), 6.

21. Hall, *The Cross in Our Context,* 195.

22. Hall, *Thinking the Faith,* 74.

23. Hall, *The Cross in Our Context,* 55.

24. Ibid., 137.

25. Ibid., 137.

26. Ibid., 40–41.

27. Describing the marks as word, sacrament, and "mutual conversation and consolation among the brothers and sisters," these authors emphasize the importance of the church as a gathered body of believers. Richard H. Bliese and Craig Van Gelder, eds., *The Evangelizing Church: A Lutheran Contribution* (Minneapolis: Augsburg Fortress, 2005).

28. "The church is the assembly of saints in which the gospel is taught purely and the sacraments are administered rightly." Robert Kolb and Timothy J. Wengert, eds., *The Book of Concord: The Confessions of the Evangelical Lutheran Church* (Minneapolis: Fortress Press, 2000), 43.

1

Deliberate Disestablishment

On summer vacations when Annie was a young girl, she attended her grandmother's nondenominational church.[1] *During one visit, Annie remembered being invited to come to the altar rail with her whole family so the pastor could pray and lay hands on her cousin with cerebral palsy. Soon after, the pastor turned to Annie and asked her how she felt at the altar. Annie recalls saying to the pastor, with gratitude, "I feel like someone has poured warm maple syrup all over me." The experiences at her grandmother's church varied dramatically from Annie's home church. Baptized Russian Orthodox, Annie and her family left their home church when they found out their priest was having an affair. At age nine, Annie not only left that church but also stopped going to church altogether, except for weddings and funerals and the occasional visit to her grandmother's church.*

Annie arrived fifteen minutes early for our interview, assuming she was late. She and the pastor had scheduled the interview early so that she would arrive on time. Annie beamed with a huge youthful smile when she realized their plan had worked. A baker at a local grocery store, Annie was an eager conversation partner, speaking openly about her life and, in particular, her experiences with Seekers, a group that is part of the newcomer welcome ministry of a small Lutheran congregation in northeastern Pennsylvania.

Annie describes her life of twenty-seven years as filled with bad luck. The man she had been dating for quite some time lapsed into a drug problem. She wanted to talk to her family but couldn't bring herself to tell them what was going on in her life. Annie went to her boyfriend's mother, and for a time, his mother tried to be unbiased and concerned for both of them. But recently, Annie felt as though what she thought and what she did weren't good enough in his mother's eyes. One Saturday evening, Annie was driving home from work. "I couldn't take it anymore," she said. "I was driving by this church on the way home, and I saw 'Saturday services.' I work every Sunday, so I said, 'I gotta do it, I gotta do it. I need something.' I was at my wit's end, and I needed something, so I stopped in because I was thinking there would be a lot of people and it started at 6:15."

Annie was wrong. The Saturday-evening service at this church averages anywhere from five to fifteen people. When Annie arrived that evening, two people in addition to the pastor welcomed her to worship. Annie was awed by their welcome and by the sermon, which she felt spoke directly to her that evening. She said, "I just basically came here because I needed peace." Peace and a friendly welcome were what she found.

Within a few weeks, Annie was asking how she could become a member. Her pastor responded, "We have a way." Annie's enthusiasm for peace and a sense of belonging drew her into the newcomer-welcoming process immediately. She talks about her arrival as perfect timing. A new six-week course on Lutheranism was beginning, the Seekers group was meeting regularly, and Confirmation[2] was scheduled within a few months at the Easter Vigil.[3] Describing her interest in faith as going "full force," Annie actively attended the Lutheran Course and biweekly meetings with the Seekers group of three or four members led by a facilitator called a catechist. "My Tuesdays are booked through May," Annie said.

In our interview, Annie explained, "I'm excited to do this. I said to my family and my friends . . . , 'This is the first thing in my life that I'm actually doing on my own that I'm excited about.' Sure, I married and I divorced, but everything else was for everyone else. This is the first thing I'm doing actually for myself. School, you have to do. It's not for you unless you go to college. Marriage you do because you want to do . . . but . . . I knew it was the wrong thing to do. Everyone was all . . . 'You're getting married—you are going to be responsible—you're going to have stability' [laughter]—so wrong about that. That's the biggest . . . I wish I could go back in time and change that one."

Annie has one friend who has attended this church with her. Her friend encouraged her to slow down and look at other churches before she joined this Lutheran congregation, a small union church that shares its building with a United Church of Christ congregation[4] and worships an average of seventy-five every weekend. Even under pressure from her friend, Annie emphasized that she is happy. She recalled, "I feel very warm here—similar to my grandmother's church. I love her church, but it's not like here. This is 'my church.'"

That Sunday evening when Annie arrived, a typical worship service was about to begin with three people gathered. This small, rural, Lutheran church is not the kind of congregation we might think would attract a twenty-seven-year-old. Annie, however, recalls that she was drawn into this particular church on her way home from work on a specific day in her life, and the three other people gathered around word and sacrament were exactly the kind of Christian community she needed. They extended to her the promise of presence: "We are here, waiting for you to arrive." Annie's congregation did not ignore the questions that brought her there. They welcomed her that night and asked her directly, "Who are you?" They entertained Annie's questions. The Seekers group within their newcomer-welcoming process invited her to explore her faith in light of her current crisis, helped her to go on as a disciple of Jesus Christ in the midst of her struggles, and courageously stayed present to Annie's suffering.

When I visited with the Seekers group as a researcher, one characteristic of the group caught my attention. When the Seekers get together, they laugh. Joanne, the catechist, shared with me just how intensely she prepares for the meeting. She consults curriculum resources, visits websites, and seeks advice from the pastor. However, once she arrives for the Seekers' scheduled time together, she invites the group to pay attention to the person who wants or needs to share an experience or story. No one, not Annie or other members of Seekers, could tell me exactly what happens when they meet, but they all feel deeply satisfied from the encounter—and laughter was a common theme.

During a meal I shared with a few members of this group, I was able to glimpse what Annie must have felt in her encounter. We shared a lot of laughter. And although the group members answered my research questions, I was keenly aware that what they wanted to learn about was *me*—the newcomer in their midst. In their focus on the newcomer, the dynamics of "inside the group" and "outside the group" disappeared. I didn't feel like a newcomer, and the group members didn't feel like longtime established members of a church I was researching. I was drawn into their center even as they were drawn to my periphery. I could sense an overwhelming identification with them while also recognizing my distinctiveness. I maintained their identity as research subjects. They maintained my identity as a researcher with questions to ask. In the coming months and years as I reflected on Annie's experience and my own, I tried to make sense of it and to put a name to the complex components that made up interactions between the Seekers and newcomers.

I had interviewed participants in newcomer-welcoming processes before encountering Annie and the Seekers, and I interviewed others after. The seamless interaction between Annie as a newcomer and the established members of her congregation was not a universal experience. I sensed deep frustration in one pastor's voice when he told me that older members of the congregation were upset that he was spending time with newcomers. An impromptu interview with a longtime volunteer in the church office confirmed this tension, as newcomers were described as the "inside group" greatly favored by the pastor. In another congregation, separate newcomer gatherings became cliques that excluded other members of the congregation. Members began asking questions such as "Why are they so special?" and "What makes them better than the rest of us?" During my conversations with members of congregations, I heard conflicting statements. Established members had the desire to welcome newcomers and even perceived themselves as very welcoming, but as efforts to design intentional newcomer-welcoming processes proceeded, some established members could not help but feel neglected and even abandoned. The process I hope to introduce is one that takes seriously this sense of feeling neglected among established members, while also insisting on the necessity of deliberately designing processes to welcome newcomers.

Why was Annie's experience so different? The difference, it seems to me, lies in the congregation's relationship to *establishment*. An established congregation is intentionally equipped to care for established members. An established congregation seeks to reduce the tension between established members and newcomers by rushing to make newcomers members. In contrast, a disestablished congregation is intentionally equipped to care for the interactions between newcomers and established members. Soon I will say more about what this disestablished congregation looks like. First, however, I turn to the nature of established congregations.

Defining Establishment

What does it mean for congregations to be established? Christendom arose in the fourth century and has remained the most influential and integral force in the history of Christianity. The radical shift from persecuted church to public church, from familial and intimate gatherings to established institutions lasted through the Middle Ages, the Reformation, and the periods of global transformation in the fifteenth through seventeenth centuries (also known as colonialization) to the organization of congregations in the United States. It might seem strange to talk about the establishment of churches in the United States, because this country was largely instituted in opposition to any federal establishment of religion—that is, supporting churches with taxes or expecting citizens to be church members without necessarily joining. The First Amendment of the Constitution of the United States of America states, "Congress shall make no law respecting an establishment of religion, or prohibiting the free exercise thereof; or abridging the freedom of speech, or of the press; or the right of the people peaceably to assemble, and to petition the Government for a redress of grievances."[5]

However, there is a distinction between a church established by the government and a culturally established church. Although the Christian church and religions in the United States were legally disestablished from the federal government and over time from the state governments as well, theologian Douglas John Hall notes that culturally, ideationally, and socially, Christian congregations were heavily established. Hall insists that our casual sneer at Europe's state church system causes us to be blind to the deep cultural establishment of the church in North America:

> In reality, what is with us is, from one point of view, (de jure) nonestablishment; but, from another point of view, it is (de facto) the most deeply entrenched kind of establishment. Relatively speaking, Christian churches in North America are independent of the state. However, in the depth of their social relationships and cultural assumptions, they are bound to the dominant culture. Establishment here is not a matter of taxes, official appointments, and ceremony (though, to a certain extent, it is also that) so much as it is of a fundamental unity with the established culture, a unity at the level of decisive values and goals. It is real establishment that is in so many ways more effective than the merely legal ones that somehow persist in Europe.[6]

The cultural establishment of the church of which Hall writes is clearly recognizable in a brief review of the history of church and culture in the mid- and late-twentieth-century United States. The widely accepted civic uses of religious imagery dramatically increased in the early 1950s as an ideological weapon in the Cold War against "godless" communism. The National Day of Prayer and the National Prayer Breakfast were instituted in the early 1950s, around the same time as "under God" was inserted into the Pledge of Allegiance. Religious language and practice came to be part of what it meant to be a patriotic American. From the 1950s through the early 1980s, Sunday mornings were a sacrosanct time set aside for rest, worship, and family. Restaurants, stores, youth athletic leagues, employers, and television programmers largely did not compete with church for the Sunday-morning attention of Americans. So-called blue laws in some states forbade (and continue to forbid) the sale of alcohol on Sundays. Prayer in public schools—even sectarian prayer, such as the Lord's Prayer and prayer in Jesus' name—was widespread. The church's needs, from issues of morality to issues of scheduling, were largely supported by the broader culture and at times the legal structures of our nation. In sum, North American congregations in the middle and latter part of the twentieth century had a far different experience than the church's situation as often portrayed in the Bible and early church history. Rather than conduct their ministry in settings hostile to their message, these congregations ministered in settings that supported and welcomed their presence. And though there was surely *some* reduction in the cultural support of religious practice in the late twentieth century (look at the rise of Sunday-morning youth athletic leagues, for example), Hall's words written in 1976 describe the undeniably privileged place the Christian church continues to occupy in American culture today. Hall purports further in his book written twenty years later, "In short, our New World variety of Christian establishment has the enormous staying power that it has because it is part and parcel of our whole inherited system of meaning, a system combining Judeo-Christian, Enlightenment, Romantic-idealist, and more recent nationalistic elements so intermingled that even learned persons have difficulty distinguishing them."[7]

Far too often, mainline congregations have carried the banner of optimism, what Hall calls "accentuating the positive":[8] "The more chaotic and threatening public life becomes, the more these churches are called upon to exemplify the conventional verities, or what are perceived as such; above all, they are looked to for order and decency, some sense of form, ritual, calm, communality."[9] Our idyllic mainline Protestant "faith communities" are safe havens for the upper- to middle-class and in many cases white membership within their walls. This posture has informed and shaped the theological perspective of the Triune God as one who keeps us safe from the chaos of the world, protecting us with power and strength. It is this posture that adapts itself to established members. It is from this posture that an inadequate relationship has emerged between congregations and "culture." Our congregations have turned in upon themselves, becoming static, protective enclaves.

THE POWER OF CULTURAL ESTABLISHMENT

So it is from a position of cultural establishment (or one of attempting to regain a 1950s-era cultural establishment) that many of our churches today conduct their ministry. Having been formed by their mid-twentieth-century experiences of establishment, of cultural support for their presence and work, congregations and denominations largely lack the tools or practices necessary to minister without the culture's supporting role. Hence, we should not be surprised to see battles in the culture war being waged by church leaders who seek to position culture into a posture favorable to the church on the one hand or unfavorable on the other. The symbiotic nature between mainline Protestant churches in North America and their cultural surroundings rendered any focus on evangelism or educating newcomers unnecessary for most of the twentieth century.

ESTABLISHMENT EVANGELISM

Evangelism within the established church is not really necessary. With cultural support of Protestant congregations and their symbiotic nature, it appears as though Christianity is everywhere. Thus, evangelism committees of mainline Protestant congregations often limit their work to publishing advertisements and managing new-member classes, rarely engaging in more direct witnessing, person-to-person evangelism, or catechetical instruction efforts for newcomers. The assumption is that the people whom mainline Protestant churches are seeking to reach are already baptized Christians. These congregations do not need to evangelize newcomers as much as they need to market the organization to them. At most, we need to Christianize Christendom as the Reformers wanted, by encouraging individuals like Annie to find their way back to the fold.[10] Such a methodology leads toward a goal of numbers accumulation and membership rolls expansion, with much less consideration given to the transformative nature of the *ecclesia crucis* gathering around word and sacrament or to the convicting and compelling power of God's word. Organizational growth is a hallmark concern of establishment congregations.

Lutheran and other mainline Protestant congregations usually have an evangelism committee made up of members. Existing under many names, depending on the congregation's relationship to "evangelism," this committee and more specifically the people who serve on this committee are charged with the dual task of encouraging the congregation to "share their faith" and reaching out to and receiving newcomers. In most cases, the task of encouraging evangelizing among the members is neglected in light of the very specific tasks of coordinating publicity outside the congregation, organizing greeters and strategies for identifying visitors, conducting new-member classes for prospective members, following up with new-member assimilation and spiritual-gifts inventories after the class, and finally, in some congregations, also looking out for inactive members. In response to the reduction of evangelism to a committee, Craig Nessan, Professor of Contextual Theology at Wartburg Seminary, has proclaimed "the death of evangelism":

By this we mean that the prevailing opinion about evangelism as one program in the church, among many other programs, must die. Evangelism has been reduced to one function of ecclesial existence and to the work of a committee alongside many other committees. In the worst-case scenario, evangelism has been reduced to an activity used to prop up the survival of the institutional church. Only when we begin to worry about church attendance or finances do we begin to consider the need for evangelism. The deeply rooted conviction that evangelism is an optional program of the church must die.[11]

What Nessan is naming, along with others who have been reinvestigating the call to mission and evangelizing, is the breakdown of cultural establishment.

ESTABLISHMENT CHRISTIAN EDUCATION

In the same way that evangelizing methodologies often focus on the Reformation principles of Christianizing Christendom, in an establishment congregation, Christian educators give sole focus to educating Christians. In fact, it is rare to find a mainline Protestant congregation in which newcomer welcome is situated as a task of the Christian education committee. In Christian education's least dynamic form, congregations teach (children mainly) the biblical principles of being kind to others through deeds by living a good Christian moral life as witness to the world, hoping that if the children are caught, Christianity will be re-rooted in North America. Often relegated to a committee in establishment congregations, Christian education might also be led by a director of Christian education or volunteer Sunday school superintendent. Sunday school (for children), confirmation instruction (particularly for adolescents), Bible study and perhaps a forum (for adults) usually take place within a classroom setting. Largely curriculum-oriented or expert-driven Christian education programs teach the Bible, catechism, worship life of the church, and perhaps some church history.

For the younger age levels in particular, education serves in part to prepare one for full membership into the organization/congregation. For instance, it was common for early- and mid-twentieth-century Lutheran churches to examine each confirmand publicly before the whole congregation, prior to the rite of confirmation (and, thus, prior to acceptance as a full member). However important, well, and good this type of education for children and adolescents is—and today, "traditional" classroom education is too often dismissed, much to the church's detriment—it is overwhelmingly bent toward the goal of full membership in the local congregation and (to some extent) the wider denomination. That is, education too often resembles a program of information-saturation transmission and is treated as a check box toward fulfilling adolescent rites of passage. Too often, the quality of education programs drops off after confirmation, that is, after one has become an "official" or "established" member of the congregation.

The ministry programs of establishment congregations do not expect actually to minister to non-Christians. These ministries are often ill equipped to articulate the Christian faith in an apologetic fashion, or speak to the truth claims of the faith with any conviction or certitude, perhaps because the leaders and members themselves have rarely had to do so. More often than not, mainline churches are equipped to describe themselves in terms of what they are *not*: how they are not like the Roman Catholics or the Evangelicals, or even how Lutherans are not quite like the Methodists or the Presbyterians (for example). But rarely are our churches able to speak affirmatively with clarity about who and what they *are* as the *ecclesia crucis*.

Again, they can hardly be blamed in one sense, because for several generations, leaders have guided the church in an era of cultural establishment, of assuming to operate in a Christian culture. When the church operates in a Christian culture (or under the assumption of a Christian culture), the art of articulating Christian identity and meaning becomes unnecessary and unpracticed. Mainline churches have operated as low-threshold membership organizations for several generations now, failing to be unique places of faith-based meaning making and discipleship formation. Because of this cultural positioning, church leaders and members are rarely in a position to speak of their faith or Christian vocation in terms meaningful to a nonbeliever. Assuming a Christian cultural context in which to conduct Christian ministry, mainline Christians are largely not practiced in the art of speaking of faith in ways that make sense to the nonbeliever—or to the newcomer whose prior experience of church may have been sporadic attendance at Sunday school twenty years earlier (see Annie).

EDUCATING NEWCOMERS

Only nine percent of mainline Protestant congregations educate their newcomers,[12] let alone welcome or encourage their participation. When these congregations do practice newcomer education, it is often a few meetings with the pastor, oriented around the local congregation's traditions, customs, and structure. The pastor may also discuss the congregation's life together, describe why certain worship practices are done in the way they are, outline his or her theological perspective, introduce the staff or congregational leaders, and finally, give a tour of the physical plant. Once they have completed this process, the baptized newcomers are welcomed to join the congregation as full members through an Affirmation of Baptism rite. If any newcomers are unbaptized, they would be baptized during a worship service. Protestant congregations accept newcomers "straight off the street into full membership."[13] This happens because there is no distinction between the cultural practices of Christianity established in North America per se and Christianity practiced within a particular congregation.

This is not the case for all congregations. Nancy Ammerman explains that, while many Protestant congregations accept an inquirer "straight off the street," sectarian groups (e.g., Jehovah's Witness, Latter-Day Saints) have intense periods of membership education prior to initiation, and conservative congregations (e.g., American Baptists, Brethren, Assemblies of God) initially accept the newcomer and follow up immediately with a process of "discipleship."[14] The discipleship process in Evangelical churches often includes a period in which new converts are shepherded by experienced members. Sectarian groups and conservative congregations tend to highlight differences in their relationship with culture, demanding transformation within the newcomer. Within Ammerman's research, Roman Catholic congregations and Orthodox communities are the most likely to host membership education (44 percent do so), followed by African American Protestant congregations, at 30 percent.[15] The point does not need to be belabored; the existence of these more elaborate or more intensive initiation practices indicates that Roman Catholic, Orthodox, and African American Protestant congregations clearly do not see themselves as part of the established culture.

How might established mainline Protestant congregations respond to their waning cultural establishment? A congregation might simply ignore it. Or a congregation might, like the sectarian religious groups noted in the previous paragraph, highlight differences in relationship to culture. Is there another way? From 2005 to 2006, I engaged in a qualitative research study exploring the newcomer-welcoming process of eight churches in the Evangelical Lutheran Church in America (ELCA). Annie's congregation was one of these eight. All eight congregations choose to recover the ancient practice of the catechumenate as their process for welcoming newcomers. These congregations were opting to respond constructively to the waning cultural establishment, instead of ignoring it. I was intrigued and sought to find out what was going on.[16]

Briefly, the catechumenate process in the ELCA is modeled after the Roman Catholic initiation process called the Rite of Christian Initiation of Adults (RCIA). In ELCA congregations, the catechumenate is a newcomer-welcoming process that consists of four distinct periods: inquiry, catechumenate, baptism, and baptismal living.[17] A liturgical rite that takes place during the congregation's worship service marks each period. These rites include welcome, enrollment, baptism, and sometimes a rite of affirmation of Christian vocation. A similar process to prepare newcomers who have been baptized and are seeking affirmation of baptism for reception into a membership, restoration to membership, or reaffirmation at a life transition involves four periods: inquiry, affirmation, candidacy, and baptismal living.[18] The rite of baptism would be adapted to a rite of affirmation of baptism for this process. This second process, adapted directly from the catechumenate, is more commonly practiced in ELCA congregations, since adult baptisms are not very common.[19]

During the initial period, called inquiry, the newcomer (inquirer) is matched with a sponsor—a baptized Christian who walks alongside the inquirer as mentor and model of the faith, encouraging the inquirer to ask questions about faith, religion, and spiritual experience. A catechist, generally also a layperson, walks alongside the inquirer and the sponsor, serving as a teacher and model of the faith. During this first period, the inquirer meets with his or her sponsor as often as possible and participates in worship, small-group Bible studies that include prayer, and other fellowship and service events of the faith community.

When inquirers begin to ask deeper questions related to faith and specific questions related to the story of Jesus Christ, they become catechumens. This second period is also open-ended and is called specifically the catechumenate or affirmation. The deeper, more specific questions of the individual are addressed in small groups with other newcomers and/or together with pastors, sponsors, and catechists. The catechumen continues to participate in worship, Bible studies with prayer, and other fellowship and service events of the congregation. The third period within the process is an intense period of baptismal preparation or candidacy that engages some of the documents of the Christian Faith, including the creeds, catechisms, and confessions. This third period often occurs (although not necessarily) during the weeks of Lent leading up to the Easter Vigil, at which the newcomer is baptized or affirmed.[20] The final period, historically called *mystagogy*,[21] occurs throughout the fifty days of Pentecost. The Lutheran catechumenate resources emphasize this period as baptismal living: "a life-long period during which the newly baptized grow more deeply into the practice of faith and Christian life."[22] During this period, the newly baptized and newly affirmed are encouraged to reflect upon their experience and their vocational identity as shaped by the Christian faith, Christian practices, and daily dying and rising. Following this ancient pattern of the catechumenate, congregations have a basic structure to help established members focus on and orient around welcoming the newcomer to Christ and Christian faith, encouraging newcomer catechesis and participation, and supporting the newcomer's ongoing life of faith lived out daily in the world.

As I learned about this process, I imagined its potential as a deliberate and structured newcomer-welcoming process for the ELCA. The more time I spent with catechumenate congregations and practitioners, the more I became fascinated with the language developing around its adaptation, particularly in regard to the theological discourse. For example, catechumenate practitioners consistently encourage congregations to be *countercultural*. Practitioners describe the catechumenate of the early church as a lengthy process of Christian initiation developed during the period of Christian persecution when Christian conversion was thoroughly countercultural. So, too, catechumenate practitioners make direct analogies between the early church and the situation of today's church, noting the need for the membership's distinct identity as disciples of Jesus who are equipped for life and ministry in the face of growing secularism[23] (or, more accurately, the reduction of Christian cultural establishment). For catechumenate practitioners, the catechumenate provides a distinguishing mark in an otherwise indistinguishable posture of Christianity within Christendom. The catechumenate, no longer responding to martyrdom in the face of persecution, gives attention to the supreme countercultural practice of reading the Bible as a story of death and resurrection with ultimate meaning for our lives in the face of a death-denying culture.[24] The catechumenate offers "a way" to break down false ideologies that the prevailing culture tries "to sell" and instill the possibility of life abundant under the cross.[25] This way provides a countercultural Christian community's experience of God.

While I do like the language of "recognizing false ideologies and idolatries," I do not like the language of counterculture or alternative. To be countercultural is not the ideal posture of the Christian congregation—quite the contrary. The posture of the people under the cross is to be a movement that engages the world with suffering love. Furthermore, the rhetoric of counterculture has unintentionally (or perhaps intentionally) led some catechumenate congregations to an "insiders versus outsiders" posture with regard to newcomer versus established members and the church versus the world's culture. Established members are protected from a chaotic outside culture and thus represent something counter to all that is outside, including the newcomer. Or at the very least, the newcomer is held in suspicion until the tension between promise and question is reduced. To define Christianity as alternative or counter to everything else is an oversimplification.[26]

THE TASK OF WELCOMING NEWCOMERS

It should be considered also that most established members on the inside of congregations do not stay there throughout the week. Congregations are not ascetic monasteries. Rather, established members move in and out of the congregation, participating in the world *and* in the church. The *ecclesia crucis* is a movement. The movement of the *ecclesia crucis* is relational—it needs the world—and only gains its identity in the task of relating to the world. But this movement is not away from the world; it is engagement with the world. The countercultural approach often leads to the church's disengagement from the world without the possibility for reengaging as a movement turned toward the world in suffering love. What is needed is an approach that urges congregations not to be countercultural in a way that creates insiders and outsiders. Congregations cannot oppose established members and newcomers or the church and the world, but must articulate the need for both.

Welcoming newcomer questions within the *ecclesia crucis* occurs at the boundary of the church and the world. A Christian identity is not static, just as the *ecclesia crucis* is not static. A Christian identity is fluid and negotiated in relation to the promise of God and what is going on in the here and now. Together with theologian Katherine Tanner, I recommend that to steer clear of the poles of asceticism (withdrawal/countercultural) on the one hand and indistinguishability (symbiotic relationship/Christendom) on the other, discipleship in the twenty-first century needs to be a task in and of itself.[27] The task is to learn how to be a disciple of Jesus Christ through Christian practices. A cruciform catechesis is learning that arises from newcomers and established members participating together in Christian discipleship practices.

In her book *Theories of Culture*, Tanner maps the influence of modern anthropology on theology, believing that theology should take into account the new directions in the postmodern study of culture in anthropology.[28] Cultures are less and less self-contained and clearly bounded units, internally consistent, and unified wholes of beliefs and values simply transmitted to all members of their respective groups as principles of social order. Rather, cultures are more and more interactive processes, fragmented, negotiated, indeterminate, conflictual, and porous. When modern anthropology sees culture as bounded, fixed, integrated, united, and holistic in meaning and identity, it is easy to embody a countercultural approach that pulls the outsider to the inside to reduce any tension. A postmodern anthropology stresses much of the opposite, highlighting the porous nature of culture and the negotiation of meaning within conflict that erupts within relationships.

Tanner sees the distinction between modern and postmodern conceptions of culture most clearly when Christians gather around discipleship practices. She argues convincingly that if Christians all have to agree on the theological essentials of practice before participating in a practice, we will never get to practicing what it means to be Christian or have anything concrete to teach our children. Rather, what is important is that we share the sense of figuring out what discipleship is. Christians are unified "by the effort Christians make to proclaim and be the disciples of God's Word—a unity of task and not necessarily of accomplishment."[29] As with building sand castles, we find joy in the task of building the castle, not in its completion. Discipleship is not a goal in and of itself; rather, discipleship occurs in the ongoing task within Christian practices of faith meeting doubt, hope meeting despair, and love meeting the suffering world. Christianity as a task neither resists being defined as countercultural nor seeks Christendom establishment. "Instead Christianity has its identity as a task. Christianity has its identity in the form of a task of looking for one."[30]

Noting the way subaltern groups adopt and change the ideals and practices of dominant groups Tanner suggests, "Differences between ways of life are often therefore established by differences of use and not by the distribution of entirely discrete cultural forms to one side or the other of a cultural boundary. Cultural difference is more a matter of how than of what; it is not so much what cultural materials you use as what you do with them that establishes identity."[31] When newcomers and established members practice discipleship, they are not creating discrete cultural forms, but using cultural materials in a certain way that matters for Christian discipleship. For instance, the practice of contemplative prayer shifts when situated in a Christian community, even though it might appear to be similar to the meditation practice within a Buddhist community. Or a moment of silence situated in a public forum is significantly different from silent prayer situated before Bible study in the congregation, even though it might be perceived as the same. Christians and non-Christians alike might share the cultural materials within these practices, but Christians situate and frame cultural materials in relation to the source and norm of faith, and different Christians bring to these practices local and distinct narratives. To participate in

Christian discipleship practices, newcomers need to learn the local elements of a practice, its resources (materials), frameworks, and perceptions.

But lest we imagine there is no distinguishing factor between Christian and non-Christian practices, it is important to clarify what a boundary looks like in a postmodern understanding of culture. The "distinctiveness of a Christian way of life is not so much formed by the boundary as *at it*."[32] When established members recognize their Christian way of life is distinct from other cultural, religious, and congregational ways of life, newcomers' questions are inevitably expected and anticipated. The Seekers recognized the boundary and anticipated Annie's questions. At the boundary, the Seekers and Annie constructed a distinctive Christian identity with one another through the task of looking for one.

DEFINING DISESTABLISHMENT

In his book *The End of Christendom and the Future of Christianity*, Hall proposes that congregations take an active role in the reduction of Christian cultural establishment, rather than passively letting this reduction occur at the expense of a more precipitous decline in membership. Congregations need to disestablish themselves through active disengagement from dominant culture:[33]

> Concretely speaking, Christians must learn how to distinguish the Christian message from the operative assumptions, values, and pursuits of our host society, and more particularly those segments of our society with which, as so-called mainstream churches, we have been identified. Because most of the denominations in question are bound up with middle-class Caucasian, and broadly liberal elements of our society, what we have to learn is that the Christian message is not just a stained-glass version of the worldview of that same social stratum.[34]

I appreciate Hall's use of the word *distinguish*, which is a recognition of the boundary. But I am not comfortable with Hall's proposal for congregations to disengage in order to reengage in order to become "the cruciform body of Jesus Christ, a priestly and prophetic community of 'the Way.'"[35] Disengagement is too close to "countercultural." Taking a cue from Tanner and recognizing that Hall's proposal to disengage uses a modern approach to culture as a boundaried whole, which is not realistic, I'd like to reverse Hall's proposal: Christian congregations need only engage, and that engagement happens through the welcome of newcomer questions.

Notice that engagement is not simply engagement of the newcomer who walks through the door, but engagement with the newcomer's questions. These questions represent more than questions, as they include the newcomer's life story, desires, hopes, and pain. Engagement is also welcoming the questions of the very newcomer who shows up, not the newcomer the congregation anticipates will show up once the leaders get their brochure, tour, and welcome committee in place. (I contend that most congregations miss opportunities to meet all the ones who actually show up while evangelism committees are perpetually getting ready.)

Tanner speaks of engagement as disarticulation. This disarticulation begins within the newcomer's questions that expose differences of interpretation among Christians themselves, not to mention between Christians and non-Christians: "Christian practices cannot take up the elements of another way of life as they form a whole; a different use of them requires a form of selective attention by which they are wrested out of their usual contexts in another way of life. They must be disarticulated, so to speak, taken apart in order to be put together again in a new way, to form a new pool of associations or a new organization of elements with weightings different from what they had elsewhere."[36] Tanner insists that the identity of Christianity should be summed up as an *unanswerable question*. And, I would add, the unanswerable question is embodied in the ever-present presence of the newcomer's question. Christian discipleship practices ought to be

> a genuine community of argument, one marked by mutual hearing and criticism among those who disagree, by a common commitment to mutual correction and uplift, in keeping with the shared hope of good discipleship, proper faithfulness, and purity of witness. This is the sort of unity of mutual admonition and concern that one finds in the letters of Paul. It is something like what Augustine talked about as the new Christian virtue of sociability: a solidarity of love and common hope, which eschews compulsion by allowing all decisions to be free, a community ruled by humility and not by way of the advantage of superior power.[37]

Following this line of thought, Christian discipleship practices are not established productions; rather, "they are always prone to dissolution, to be taken apart, reorganized, and their elements reinterpreted in the process."[38]

With joy the ecclesia crucis entertains the unanswerable question, eagerly taking up the task of figuring out what a Christian identity looks like through discipleship practices.

THE POWER OF DISESTABLISHMENT

Now we can identify the difference between congregations that, like Annie's, welcome newcomers and their disarticulations around Christian practices and congregations that are struggling with the awkward relationship between established members and newcomers. The latter congregations are using the catechumenate as a deliberate newcomer-welcoming process in established ways to preserve the static nature of the church, reducing the tension that exists when newcomers are present. In the worst case, established members take sides for or against newcomers. In Annie's congregation, the catechumenate was a ministry of welcoming newcomers that facilitated Annie's participation in discipleship practices and where established members were drawn toward Annie through her questions.

Newcomer disarticulation around Christian practices together with established members becomes the site of creative theological judgment. Active and deliberative disestablishment is engagement, welcoming newcomers (and their questions) to participation in the practices of discipleship within the congregation. Disestablishment is welcoming disarticulations within the *ecclesia crucis*. The *ecclesia crucis* is church when it is practicing the confession of faith, hope, and love, welcoming newcomers into discipleship practices where faith meets doubt, hope meets despair, and love meets the suffering world. A cruciform catechesis occurs in the tension between question and promise, ultimately reengaging the congregation in the world.

The Seekers in their identification with Annie engaged their own doubts, came face-to-face with their own despair, and saw incarnate before them the suffering world. Week after week, with Joanne's careful preparation, they came together to discuss the Bible, pray with one another, share in Christian conversation, worship weekly on Sundays with the larger congregation, and together discern their Christian identity in relation to Annie and indeed to one another. Around the deliberate practice of welcoming newcomers, the established members and even the wider community that professed faith in Jesus Christ stepped into Annie's doubt. They engaged the despair and suffering of Annie and the world by engaging her questions with faith, hope, and love.

Notes

1. All the names of research participants have been changed. Annie's story comes from my research for the Faithful Practices Project at Princeton Theological Seminary between 2002 and 2004. More details about my research design can be found in the appendix.

2. The pastor told me later that what Annie described as "confirmation" was going to be the Affirmation of Baptism rite within the Lutheran Church. Two high school boys were going to be "confirmed" with the Affirmation of Baptism rite at the Easter Vigil. It was easier for Annie to describe the rite as confirmation rather than "affirmation of baptism," particularly since Annie had never been confirmed in the Russian Orthodox Church. This rite and opportunity meant a great deal to her.

3. The Easter Vigil is dramatic worship with three movements: light and readings, baptism and the remembrance of baptism, and a Holy Communion Mass. The vigil is kept on the eve of Easter. Worship begins with the congregation gathered outside in darkness of the night. A bonfire is lit to represent Christ's light coming in the midst of darkness into the world. The congregation moves from the bonfire to a worship space in which twelve pericopes from the Hebrew and New Testaments are read. After the readings, the congregation moves to the font to celebrate the baptism of a catechumenal candidate and/or remember the baptism of all who are gathered. The baptism is followed by the Easter acclamation that Christ has risen, and the worship space is fully lit and decorated with Easter lilies as the congregation proceeds with the readings for Easter Day, a sermon, and celebration of the sacrament of Holy Communion. In some congregations, these movements occur in a different order.

4. While the union has been active for nearly a hundred years, the churches are becoming increasingly independent of one another.

5. Constitution of the United States, Amendment I.

6. Douglas John Hall, *Lighten Our Darkness: Toward an Indigenous Theology of the Cross* (Philadelphia: Westminster, 1976), 48.

7. Douglas John Hall, *The End of Christendom and the Future of Christianity*, Christian Mission and Modern Culture, ed. Alan Neely, H. Wayne Pipkin and Wilbert R. Shenk (Valley Forge, PA: Trinity Press International, 1997), 31–32.

8. Douglas John Hall, *Confessing the Faith: Christian Theology in a North American Context* (Minneapolis: Fortress Press, 1996), 464.

9. Ibid.

10. See Scott H. Hendrix, *Recultivating the Vineyard: The Reformation Agendas of Christianization* (Louisville, KY: Westminister John Knox, 2004).

11. Craig L. Nessan, "After the Death of Evangelism: The Resurrection of an Evangelizing Church," in *The Evangelizing Church: A Lutheran Contribution*, ed. Richard H. Bliese and Craig Van Gelder (Minneapolis: Augsburg Fortress, 2005), 114.

12. Nancy Tatom Ammerman, *Pillars of Faith: American Congregations and Their Partners* (Berkeley: University of California Press, 2005), 33–35. I have no reason to believe that the membership education practice of ELCA congregations varies significantly from the figure representative of mainline congregations.

13. Ibid., 33.

14. Ibid., 33.

15. Ibid., 35.

16. I developed the framework for my research with a dual focus, attending to the catechumenate's role in the life of the congregation and the catechumenate's role in the life of the individual, whether a newcomer or an established member. Within the congregational perspective, I explored the catechumenate as an intentional process of congregational renewal fostering individual and corporate faith through catechesis and worship with the intent of strengthening an evangelizing culture and outreach beyond the church walls. In each congregation, I was eager to see how leaders welcome newcomers, how they integrated the

catechumenate into the congregation's other ministries such as Christian education and service in the world, how the role of sponsors encouraged the growth and maturity of established members in the congregation, and how the catechumenate spurred a missional or evangelizing spirit within the congregation. The second focus of my research explored the catechumenate as a newcomer-welcoming process for addressing the faith questions of newcomers as they become a part of a congregation (through baptism or affirmation of baptism) and nurturing the faith of individuals already members of a congregation (worshippers, sponsors, and catechists). To address this focus, I developed a research question with specific attention to catechetical process and development of spiritual practices within the catechumenate in congregations. My research at each congregation consisted of a semistructured interview with church leaders (pastors and associates) and catechumenate leaders (catechists), a focus group with newcomers who joined after participating in the catechumenate process, a focus group with those newcomers who decided to join without participating in the catechumenate process, and a focus group with members who participated in the catechumenate as sponsors. More details about my research design and the questions that guided the semistructured interviews and the focus groups can be found in the appendix.

17. Samuel Torvend and Lani Willis, eds., *Welcome to Christ: A Lutheran Introduction to the Catechumenate* (Minneapolis: Augsburg Fortress, 1997), 8. See also *Go Make Disciples: An Invitation to Baptismal Living* (Minneapolis: Augsburg Fortress, 2012).

18. Dennis Bushkofsky, *What Do You Seek? Welcoming the Adult Inquirer* (Minneapolis: Augsburg Fortress, 2000).

19. I am aware that liturgical historian Maxwell Johnson and others are deeply unhappy with the adaptation of the practice of the catechumenate with individuals who are already baptized. Johnson has a grave concern that there is too much confusion and not enough distinction between new converts and affirmers: "Such has led some to suggest that the real intent of the restored catechumenate in today's churches is but a new way to make 'converts' out of already baptized Christians, who seek to be received or transferred into another church." Johnson continues in a strong fashion, calling this practice lamentable. In addition, Johnson lifts up the concern of theologian Aiden Kavanagh, who said regarding this issue in 1987, "In all candor, I must confess that I give [the catechumenate] less than a fifty percent chance of success, and you will recall that I have been one of its most consistent public advocates for the past fifteen years." As much as I value the arguments made by these scholars, I do not agree with their conclusion. I believe the catechumenate is a helpful ministry for welcoming all newcomers—both the unbaptized and those affirming their faith. A modified version of RCIA is also practiced for newcomers who are already baptized. See Thomas H. Morris, *The RCIA: Transforming the Church; A Resource for Pastoral Implementation*, rev. and updated ed. (New York: Paulist, 1997).

20. If the newcomer is already baptized, this period would explore the meaning of baptism and prepare the newcomer for an Affirmation of Baptism rite at the Easter Vigil. Whether the catechumenate should be reserved for the unbaptized only is an ongoing conversation among catechumenate practitioners. See note 19.

21. *Mystagogy* was the period during which the newly baptized explored the sacraments of baptism and Holy Communion and their vocational callings in daily life.

22. Torvend and Willis, *Welcome to Christ: A Lutheran Introduction to the Catechumenate*, 8.

23. Richard Osmer and Friedrich Schweitzer offer a helpful description of secularization: "Secularization theory postulates that religious worldviews, which base their authority on tradition, have given way to purely rational and experiential types of knowing which are part and parcel of modernity." Richard R. Osmer and Friedrich Schweitzer, *Religious Education between Modernization and Globalization*, Studies in Practical Theology, ed. James W. Fowler, Don S. Browning, Friedrich Schweitzer, and Johannes A. van der Ven (Grand Rapids: Eerdmans, 2003), 57. Osmer and Schweitzer have also explored the recent critiques of secularization theory. "Scholars in various fields have recently called attention to three social phenomena that challenge secularization theory's analysis of what is happening to religion worldwide: (1) the continuing significance of what has been termed 'invisible religion,' (2) the continuing significance of

religiously motivated social movements, and (3) non-Western critiques of 'godless Western secular materialism." (57)

24. Bushkofsky, *What Do You Seek?*, 18, 20.

25. Torvend and Willis, *Welcome to Christ: A Lutheran Introduction to the Catechumenate*, 36–46.

26. I recognize that the countercultural posture is reminiscent of Richard Niebuhr's Christ against culture typology. Niebuhr recognized that this might have been the posture of the first Christians toward the world, but he also delineates this posture's inadequacies. H. Richard Niebuhr, *Christ and Culture* (San Francisco: HarperSanFrancisco, 2001), 66. See also Craig A. Carter, *Rethinking Christ and Culture* (Grand Rapids: Brazos, 2006), 42.

27. "Christianity has its identity as a task." Kathryn Tanner, *Theories of Culture: A New Agenda for Theology*, Guides to Theological Inquiry (Minneapolis: Fortress Press, 1997), 155.

28. Ibid.

29. Ibid., 136.

30. Ibid., 155.

31. Ibid., 112.

32. Ibid., 115.

33. Hall, *The End of Christendom and the Future of Christianity*, 43.

34. Ibid., 44–45.

35. Ibid., 49.

36. Tanner, *Theories of Culture*, 117–18.

37. Ibid., 123–24.

38. Ibid., 164.

2

Intersections of Inquiry

A newcomer's presence in a congregation is, in many respects, unsettling. Newcomers often exemplify the fluidity that characterizes contemporary American religious identity. Their arrival at a particular congregation is more likely about preference and choice than any immutable characteristic. Newcomers are not yet committed to be "*my* people." Oldcomers (my creative word for established members) have spent a longer period of time within the congregation and tend to reflect the static and even determined nature of religious identity. Oldcomers often assume that the beliefs and practices of a congregation mirror their religious identity in a fairly consistent way, even if this is not the case. Thus, newcomers in a congregation heighten the oldcomer's experience of hybridity because a newcomer's inquiries disturb what is believed to be settled, determined, and fixed.

LIMINALS

Fluidity characterized Annie's experience. She didn't step across the threshold of a Lutheran church out of some commitment to the Lutheran church. She walked through the doors on a Saturday night because she was at her wit's end. Annie was looking for peace. Born into the Russian Orthodox tradition, attending her grandmother's nondenominational church occasionally, and then finding herself welcomed in a Lutheran church in her twenties, Annie does not conceive of her religious identity as an immutable characteristic. Her religious identity adapts and adjusts to fit her situation. In the words of two sociologists, Annie's religious identity is "fuzzy around the edges," and she is not alone.[1]

According to sociologists Robert Putnam and David Campbell, 10 percent of every religious tradition is made up of "liminal members" (liminal is from the Latin word for "threshold"): "These folks seem to be standing at the edge of a religious tradition, half in and half out. Sometimes we catch them thinking of themselves as 'something' (Baptist or Catholic or whatever), and other times they think of themselves as 'none.'"[2] Switching between faith traditions or between denominations within the Christian family is curiously common in the United States. A report from the Pew Forum on Religion and Public Life found that 24 percent of all Americans explore different faiths regularly or occasionally.[3]

That liminal members are switching, not committing, and regularly trying something new may not be a surprise. Another statistic is more intriguing. The religious beliefs and practices of most liminals do not change even though their affiliations change. Over a two-year period that consisted of switching, liminals "prayed as often . . . , they believed in God just as fervently (or just as tentatively), they went to church virtually as often. . . . The only thing that changed was how they described their religious identity."[4] Religious practices remain consistent, religious beliefs stay the same, but religious affiliation and identity change with the wind.

What does this mean? Let's explore an example. Praying is a Christian practice. An established congregation assumes newcomers already pray consistently because of their Christian identity, even though this may or may not be true. When a newcomer joins a congregation through a three-week membership class and the newcomer's beliefs and practices around prayer are not explored explicitly, neither the newcomer nor the congregation ever learns about the other's perceptions of prayer. The newcomer's beliefs and practices essentially remain the same. If the congregation has a prayer ministry and the newcomer happens to participate in that prayer ministry, then the newcomer's belief and practice of prayer might experience significant change. It is highly unlikely, however, that a liminal who changes religious affiliation within two years will join an established prayer group. Without any explicit attention to teaching discipleship practices at the time of welcome, newcomers rarely experience any change in their beliefs and practices. In contrast, a disestablished congregation recognizes that the newcomer does not know the congregation's resources, frameworks, and perceptions for the practice of prayer, and it sets up a process for facilitating a newcomer's participation in the central practices of discipleship.

Putman and Campbell also found that the percentage of people raised without any religious affiliation, the "nones," is growing consistently. Thus, if religious practices and beliefs stay the same among people inclined toward religion, then nonreligious practices and beliefs also stay the same among those less inclined toward religion. If we place the growing number of nones alongside the statistic that the practices and beliefs of liminals do not change significantly, the reason to pay attention to how newcomers in congregations learn Christian discipleship practices and articulate beliefs is clear: when someone switches between different religious faiths and different Christian denominations or begins to explore faith again or for the first time, practices and beliefs ought to change.

LINGERING WITH LIMINALS

Before I turn toward exploring how practices and beliefs might change among liminals, I want to return to my claim in the introduction that welcoming newcomers is necessary to save the church. Through a biblical analogy of God's unique relationship with the people of Israel and a theological frame that seeks a balance between God's inclusive and exclusive relationship with God's people, I determine that the church is saved in its relationship with liminals and nones.

That Israel is God's and God is Israel's is the central promise echoing throughout the Hebrew scripture.[5] The covenant formula, "I will be your God, and you shall be my people," affirms the distinctiveness—the exclusive nature—of God's relationship with the descendants of Abraham and Sarah. God promises Abraham and Sarah to provide numerous descendants and land. These promises are personal. The exodus out of slavery in Egypt is the first decisive event in Israel's history in which God acts decisively and particularly on Israel's behalf. God chooses a side. Following the exodus, God's instructions to Moses reiterate the covenantal promise: "I will dwell among the Israelites, and I will be their God. And they shall know that I am the Lord their God, who brought them out of the land of Egypt that I might dwell among them; I am the Lord their God" (Exod. 29:45).[6]

God's promise to be in covenantal relationship with Israel is still particular even when the people turn away from that promise. In the experience of exile, God's frustration with the people of Israel is clear. Jeremiah preaches destruction, announcing to Israel and Judah that God has turned away:

> Thus says the Lord concerning this people:
> Truly they have loved to wander,
> they have not restrained their feet;
> therefore the Lord does not accept them. (Jer. 14:10a)

Less well known are the decrees of the prophet Amos. Amos's central message is death: "The end has come upon my people Israel" (Amos 8:2). Destruction is as personal as promise. Not only does Amos announce death for

God's beloved children, the prophet asks two questions unparalleled in all of scripture:[7]

> Are you not like the Ethiopians to me,
> O people of Israel? says the Lord.
> Did I not bring Israel up from the land of Egypt,
> and the Philistines from Caphtor and the Arameans from Kir? (Amos 9:7)[8]

In this particular instance, the questions arise: "Who are *my* people?" and "To whom does the promise extend?" and "Who else is included in the promise?" Do God's promises extend to the Philistines and the Arameans? Is God's election possibly something that can be experienced in a different land? According to Amos, yes.

Through Amos' inclusive announcement of God's promise, the people of Israel live the question "To whom do these promises extend?" They experience God's preferential option as broader than they could have ever imagined.[9] And more, missiologist Peter Cruchley Jones explores through Amos that exile "is not of itself a mistake best soon rectified."[10] In exile, the people of God become what the prophet Hosea metaphorically names "Lo-ammi" which means "not my people." This verse in the opening chapter of Hosea is a direct reversal of the covenantal formula, "for you are not my people, and as for me, not 'I am' to you."[11] Perhaps, as Crunchley Jones asserts, exile is a place for God's people to linger because something radical is experienced in being "not my people."

The tension between "not my people" and "my people" is heartbreaking to observe. Amos is the only prophet who maintains the pain of God's broken promise without resolving it. Hosea reverses the harsh decree immediately in the very next verse of the chapter. "Yet the number of the people of Israel shall be like the sand of the sea, which can be neither measured nor numbered; and in the place where it was said to them, "You are not my people," it shall be said to them, "Children of the living God." (Hosea 1:10) Jeremiah, the prophet of destruction, cannot bear to leave the people without a promise. He recalls the covenant between Israel and God: "But this is the covenant that I will make with the house of Israel after those days, says the Lord: I will put my law within them, and I will write it on their hearts; and I will be their God, and they shall be my people" (Jer. 31:33). Amos holds out. Mercy will come in the distant future. Until then, only faith can see hope where there is only despair, and love where there is suffering.

Jesus' own ministry stands in continuity with the prophets of Israel. And in him, we see the God of Israel. In the fifteenth chapter of Matthew's Gospel, a Canaanite woman confronts Jesus. Interpretations of this text often portray Jesus as displaying more human than godly qualities because of his dismissal of the woman's plea for her daughter. I have come to see this text differently. Here, Jesus is the God of Israel, determined to reestablish the covenant with those who had turned away from God. He responds, "I was sent only to the lost sheep of the house of Israel" (Matt 15:24). At her second request for help, he responds again, "It is not fair to take the children's food and throw it to the dogs." God's preferential option is clear. The promise is personal for Israel, and the implication is that this promise is not for her. The woman persists, "But even the dogs eat from the master's table." And in her faithful response, we can hear faint echoes of Amos: "If you, the God of Israel, can liberate the Philistines and the Arameans along with the Israelites, then you can heal a Canaanite woman's daughter." Jesus instantly recognizes her faith and heals her daughter. God's exclusive promise is extended in radically inclusive ways.

Exclusivity appears in some of the hardest texts of the New Testament. In John's Gospel, Jesus says to the disciples, and specifically to Thomas, "I am the way, the truth, and the life. No one comes to the Father except through me" (John 14:6). The disciples are perplexed and demand to see the Father. "Show us the Father, and we will be satisfied" (John 14:8). Thomas and Philip doubt even as "I Am" is standing before them. This conversation is found in chapter 14 of John's Gospel as a portion of Jesus' farewell discourse. New Testament scholar Sarah Henrich translates the first verse of this chapter with the word, "trust" instead of "believe." Jesus says, "Do not let your hearts be troubled, *trust* in God, *trust* also in me."[12] To trust Jesus is to trust the God of Israel. To see Jesus is to see the Father. To trust and see the God of Israel is to trust a God whose covenantal reach extends beyond our wildest imagination.

Theologian Paul Rajashekar recalls the old patristic dictum *extra ecclesiam nulla salus* (outside the church, there is no salvation), which among Lutherans became *extra Christum nulla salus* (outside Christ, there is no salvation).[13] Among Lutherans, this particular exclusivism is described in a hermeneutical circle of the *solas* (*sola* means "alone"): God alone, Christ alone, grace alone, scripture alone, word alone, faith alone, etc. Rajashekar explains that the *solas* create what appears to be a boundary of faith, exclusive and particular:

> In a multi-faith society, a generic affirmation of faith in 'God alone' may not meet a great resistance (except of course by atheists!). However, the Lutheran hermeneutic is not content with a theocentric view of reality that easily accommodates other religious belief in terms of grace and truth. The Lutheran view of 'God alone'

is imposed with a decisive limitation in the claim, 'Christ alone.' But this 'Christ alone' claim does not represent a 'cosmic Christ' or a 'universal logic'. Rather, it points to the historical Jesus Christ. The Lutheran way of interpreting Christ is invariably tied to *faith* in Christ, which in turn comes by hearing of the word (*ex auditu*). The *word alone* is not any word, any good word, not even the words of Scripture, but a word of promise that points to *grace alone*. The *grace alone* refers back to what God has done in and through *Christ alone*.[14]

The *solas* invite Christians to confess the promise; ultimately the cross alone is our theology. The boundary of the *solas* (or what I have been terming the promise) becomes clear only when it is met by the *simuls* (or what I might call the question), and for Rajashekar, the *simuls* are the basis for Christian engagement. The *simuls* affirm God's radical inclusive love for the world. Without the *simuls* the *solas* will turn in upon themselves and vice versa.

> Lutheran theology understands that God's revelation is simultaneously hidden and revealed; God's activity occurs simultaneously through the work of the left hand and right hand; Christ is simultaneously human and divine; the saving activity of God is simultaneously through law and gospel; the Christian is simultaneously saint and sinner; the sacrament of the bread and wine is simultaneously the body and blood; the kingdom of God is simultaneously present here and now and not yet.[15]

The *simul* approach captures the radical inclusive love God has for God's creation and enables Christians to view the world in the same way, engaging creation and culture. God's intention is for creation to be good.[16] What is good in the world is God's creative work as *larva dei*—the work of God under the mask of God. Where evil reigns in the world and where cultures and practices turn in upon themselves, God is at work making good—even within the church. Indeed, in Christ, the cosmos has been redeemed and so too the materials of culture and practices and the Holy Spirit is making the church's engagement holy. Thus, Christians can engage the world trusting that God's hidden work of redemption through the cross is present.[17] The people of the cross are called to engage in active and deliberative disestablishment, welcoming newcomers (and their questions) to participation in the practices of discipleship within the congregation. And even then, what is known about the reign of God and God's alien work is revealed only in the cross through faith.

Thus, the cross alone is our theology. God's activity looks like foolishness to the world, but through the eyes of faith it is wisdom. The only way to "learn" this life of God is to learn the practices of discipleship under the cross, experienced in the tension between question (not my people) and promise (my people).

The ancient pattern of the catechumenate is a way for both oldcomers and newcomers to share their resources, frameworks, and perceptions around central discipleship practices and mutually inform one another's practice. In relationship with one another, to "learn" this life of God is to learn the practices of discipleship under the cross, experienced in the tension between question (not my people) and promise (my people). The catechumenate takes seriously two important elements of that mutuality. First, learning to practice discipleship within a new congregation or setting takes time. What distinguishes a newcomer and an oldcomer is the amount of time spent in relation to the congregation. Newcomers and oldcomers need structured time together to learn from one another. Second, Christian discipleship is deeply connected to context. Discipleship is not an abstract set of principles. Discipleship is personal and calls upon individuals within different communities to practice discipleship differently. In this chapter, I explore the stories of three liminals and their arrivals at the threshold of congregations. I invite you to notice how facilitating their participation takes time and in what ways the invitation to discipleship is made personal within a relationship to the community.

Maly's Story

Maly and her husband, Tony, started attending a Lutheran church in my neighborhood because they desired to have their son baptized. During a prebaptismal conversation with the family, my pastor learned that Maly had never been baptized, though she was open to exploring the possibility. The pastor knew of my research area and asked me if I'd like to be involved in Maly's baptismal process as a catechist. For three months, Maly and Tony and another couple whose wife desired baptism met with sponsors, the pastor, and me as catechist to explore the Christian faith. About two weeks before Easter, Maly began to express doubts and concerns. She wasn't ready for baptism. The process had been too quick, and she needed more time. At the Easter Vigil, Maly's son was baptized, and Tony was received into membership in the congregation through affirmation of faith. In the weeks following the Easter Vigil, the pastor and I kept meeting with Maly to continue her process of inquiry.

Maly was born in the late 1970s during the height of the Khmer Rouge genocide in Cambodia. Her family immigrated to the United States in the 1980s. Maly's parents are practicing Buddhists, and Maly is the only one of her three siblings who is still Buddhist. The others have converted to Christianity. In one conversation, Maly said, "I believe my family was saved by a divine presence in Cambodia. But, I don't know what to believe about that presence. I'm listening for a voice, and I don't hear it." She continued, "Although Buddhism is good philosophy of life, it is not capable of explaining why my family survived."

For many weeks, we sat with Maly's questions, turning them over, reading Scripture, wondering, and praying aloud. Week after week, Maly shared more and more stories about the stumbling blocks preventing her from being baptized as a Christian. Many of her concerns related to Christians and their behaviors. Maly could not understand why there are so many Christians intent on condemning people to hell. Maly's Baptist boyfriend in college had told her that everyone who has not been baptized is going to hell. Maly also had a coworker who prayed for her boss's soul every day. Her boss was Jewish. When their boss was promoted out of their office, Maly's coworker let out a "Hallelujah." Hardest of all, Maly wondered about her homeland in the aftermath of the Khmer Rouge. Some of the leaders of the Khmer Rouge, while on trial for their offenses, professed to be born-again Christians. Maly could not comprehend how and why God could forgive their crimes against humanity. One evening, caught between her two faiths, she wondered aloud, "Who am I going to see when I die? My parents? Or my husband and son?"

One day after a meeting, Maly and I walked out of church together. She wondered aloud why it was even necessary to come to church. "Joel Osteen makes a lot more sense, and I can hear him on my couch," she said. As she spoke, my heart raced, because I desired for Maly to see how beautiful it is to worship with one another within our community and how much we care for each other. "Unlike Joel Osteen's worship," I said, "our congregation's worship invites us into relationship with God, with each other, and with the poor and those in need." But as I responded, Maly stared at me blankly. I began to realize something I hadn't seen before. Maybe our congregation's worship doesn't do what I said it does. At the very least, Maly certainly didn't experience worship as an encounter with God and all of God's people in the way I did. I started to panic a bit. I didn't know where to turn. Her question was deeply unsettling for me but even more concerning, I wondered, how would her question land within the congregation?

Maly's question lies at the heart of Putnam and Campbell's statistic. As a liminal, standing on the edge of two faiths, would she experience a change in her beliefs about this Christian God and in her practices of worship? The need underneath Maly's question was clear. She desired a worshipping experience that fed her weary body and soul and connected her to the divine presence that saved her family. Staying at home and watching Joel Osteen made a lot more sense as a response to her weariness and she was searching for a divine encounter within our congregation and not finding it. Maly's question unsettled me because she questioned the promise I imagined to be true. She compelled me to linger at the unsettling place of a cruciform catechesis and ask, "Where does God show up?," "What does discipleship look like when God's promises are elusive for me, for Maly, and for our congregation?" What does faithfulness in the midst of doubt look like?

The congregation in which we participated together was still quite established and equipped to care for established members. Maly's questions did not land within the congregation. Instead, our congregation assumed Maly's experience of worship would adapt to fit our "own" practice (further assuming that the congregation had only "one" particular way to worship). I quickly realized that what was happening to Maly had happened to me when I had first started to participate in the practices of this congregation. In fact, I had no idea how "our" congregation thought about worship. I could not speak for "us." I could only speak for myself. As earnest as Maly's question was, her question could not disarticulate the congregation's practice of worship, because her question, which was now also my question, remained on the street outside the church. The profound questions she asked during our conversations inside the church about the hypocrisy of Christians practicing Christianity and her internal turmoil regarding her decision to become a Christian were also relegated to the margins and experienced by very few in the congregation even though her questions are the growing norm of so many people outside of the church.

I invite you to notice that the next two stories are a bit different.

Henry's Story

Henry had been away from the church for thirty years. Although he had been raised Roman Catholic, he described spending most of his life "wandering, occasionally looking but never quite finding . . . never finding what I was looking for." At the age of forty-nine, Henry was diagnosed with terminal pancreatic cancer. At the encouragement of his doctor and some friends, he started searching for a church. He found a Lutheran church just five minutes from his house. The service felt familiar enough to his early-childhood experiences for him to enjoy it, but the pastor's preaching was what "blew him away." He described the sermons as "incredible."

More than the comforting atmosphere and the pastor's sermons, Henry was captivated by the congregation's welcome: "The first Sunday I came, not being quite aware of how things worked or anything about the Lutheran church, I came in and sat down, and I was trying to follow along. . . . One of the other members came up behind me and put his hand on my shoulder, and he handed me a program. He said, 'It's all right here.' Oh, and I said, 'Thank you; it all makes sense.'" Over time, Henry began to see differences between the Lutheran and Roman Catholic perspectives, particularly through the preaching, and felt more comfortable with Lutheran theology and "the religion piece" as a result. He noticed a bulletin announcement about "The Way," the catechumenate at this congregation, and decided to sign up.

Every Sunday evening from October through Pentecost, participants in The Way gather together. When they arrive, tables are set up for dinner. Henry recalled:

> *It's very interesting to me that that initial time at the dinner is spent just talking about your life—just "How was your week?" It's not "What happened with you and God this week?"; it's, you know, "My car did this, and the kids"—ah, you know. We've all become very close. And you know, we always sit at different tables. There's been a pretty good mix. We've had pretty good conversations. There's a trust and a community that has been built over that time. It's really nice over that dinnertime, because we are sharing ourselves—not necessarily our faith. We are building this community of new people with the catechists who are there, and our sponsors are there; everyone is there for dinner, and you are really sort of drawn in. That section has really been, looking back, has really been nice—you know, really nice. Whoever plotted this out was really wise, you know—really thinking.*

After dinner, participants in The Way move to another room, where they all sit together in a circle. There the pastors bring up the church news and discuss any important events or experiences in the lives of those participating in The Way. The leaders outline what the events are for the evening and introduce the text to be discussed. Henry described the different parts within The Way as "gaining cohesion week after week—gradually becoming routine."

The large group then divides into smaller groups of six or eight, each led by a catechist. Each group spends about forty-five minutes reading and reflecting on the gospel text appointed for the upcoming Sunday worship. Catechumens and sponsors, who are paired together by the pastors and the catechists, attend the same group with one another. Sponsors are also encouraged to meet the newcomers at other times during the week. Henry was paired with William:

> *Pastor works really hard and very carefully, and in my case, it was just a perfect match. William and I are like old buddies. We get together and just hang out—go have coffee. We get together and talk about God and religion and how it affects our lives. We also care about each other. There is a really deep relationship. It was almost instantaneous for us. We're both a little off the left of mainstream. Our lives have sort of wandered around; we've done this, and we've done that. . . . It was just an immediate [snapped his fingers] connection.*

I asked Henry whether meeting someone like William helped dispel some of the myths he might have had about the average churchgoer. He replied, "Yes. It was just like, whoa, it was just like, wow, you know; [we both had] an oddball sense of humor."

As my interview with Henry closed, I asked him to summarize his experience with The Way, and he offered this assessment:

> *You know, we have this real special community, this really special group, and all the wonderful little relationships that are being built—not just the sponsors, but everything that is going on. The chance to just be together and talk about ideas is just incredible. I wonder what will happen when The Way is finished. That will lead to something else, because there will be a hole there, and I'll need to fill it. This has built a real longing. The Way continues for a while after Easter, but I know as it comes to a close, it's going to be very sad. OK, now I'll seek something more, because it has really sparked that. The group is just a real sense of safety and security. Here is this group that I look forward to every Sunday.*

Henry noted that he really hoped to fill the hole left by the catechumenate by cooking dinners for the next year's catechumenate group. For as many church events as he can, he helps out in the kitchen. We met up again later in the week for the youth and children's program at the church. When I stood from my table to get food, he was right there in the kitchen, serving soup.

Henry's questions were profoundly simple: "Are you a people who can handle an ultimate question? Can you accompany me as I face death?" Henry's sponsor, catechists, and pastors responded with an unqualified yes. Embodying a cruciform catechesis, Henry's sponsor, William, tended the holy spaces that invited Henry to explore his doubts, his despair, and his suffering. And what happened? These holy spaces opened up the possibility for Henry's religious identity to strengthen and for his practices and his beliefs to change. Over the course of the year, Henry noted distinctions between his Roman Catholic upbringing and his current participation in a Lutheran congregation. Henry offered up these differences as a way to make crisper the fuzzy edges of his religious identity. These distinctions were not over-and-against differences, but rather particular practices and theological frameworks that made each community exceptional. An intentional welcoming process offered Henry the space to notice and name aloud these distinctions and work out his religious identity at the boundary of different Christian perspectives.

These holy spaces also held the questions of Henry's sponsor, William. And together, Henry and William encouraged each other to bear witness to faith, hope, and love, spotting these marks of Christian discipleship in their daily interactions. The relationship Henry had with William helped to demystify the stumbling blocks of Christian discipleship. With William's testimony in his ears, Henry learned to trust the diversity of perspectives about Christian faithfulness held within the congregation and Henry found his own witness. Their task together was to discern their Christian identity and to do this in relationship with Scripture, worship, service, and in relationship to one another and to the *ecclesia crucis.*

Henry and William were not alone in attending to a cruciform catechesis. Henry's participation in the catechumenate group deepened his sense of belonging and filled a space in his life he had not known existed. Because Henry had been walking with twenty other people, newcomers and oldcomers alike, all were experiencing the dying and rising of baptism with Henry. Henry's death would be their death. Henry's life would be their life. Henry's courage was their courage, and in turn, their courage was Henry's courage. Through a cruciform catechesis, this disestablished congregation held the tension between question and promise, engaging Henry's disarticulations where faith met doubt, hope met despair, and love met the suffering world through the presence of Henry and his questions.

LORI'S STORY

Lori describes herself as a rebel who spurned religion but was always interested in things spiritual. As she walked through life, she noticed, "Something in me isn't forgiven. I was a student of world religions, and I thought, 'Isn't Jesus the one who does that?' Jesus said, 'Forgiveness is yours.'" Lori found herself searching for a Christian congregation. She was not very impressed when she first arrived at her local Lutheran church, but she inquired as to how she might join. The pastor told her, "We have a way." Intrigued, Lori began the catechumenate process called The Way at this congregation. "We start with Scripture: Read it, Reflect, Read it, Apply, Read it again. Let the word work on you. Most churches say, 'Here's the story, and here's what it means.' Not here. For thinking people like me, this church asks you to turn on your brain."

Although she continued to worship, Lori dropped out of The Way within a few weeks because she thought Lutherans were too nice (she was not), too quiet (she was not), and didn't ask enough questions (she had plenty for everyone). The following year, Lori joined The Way a second time. "This time, I got stuck on the fourth commandment. I understood that it was important, but there was no way I would honor my parents. I dropped out. Still, I kept coming to church. I guess the Holy Spirit was leading that part of the process." A couple of years later, Lori joined The Way a third time. She stayed but fought the whole way through. "My questions became more and more complicated. I was a rebellious Adam, a doubting Thomas, and the woman at the well. But my sponsor and the pastor kept telling me to ask my questions. They reminded me that sometimes I'd run up against mystery. Somehow, I was comforted by this."

Lori did not know whether she had been baptized. As the period of baptismal preparation arrived, she decided to be baptized at the Easter Vigil, just to make sure. The pastor told Lori she had to find out whether or not she had been baptized. Lori remembers being angry. Still, she called her mother, who gave her a completely mixed response and said only that Lori's grandmother wanted her to be baptized. Lori also called her father, who said, "Yeah, I got stuffed into a suit for a couple of those things, but who knows who it was for." Lori decided to call her grandmother's church. She made a few phone calls, remembering that her grandmother's church had burned down, and ultimately figured out where the salvaged records had been transferred. She finally reached a church secretary. Lori recalled,

> When I told her my story, she said she knew my grandmother but had no idea whether the baptismal records had transferred after the fire. She said she was really busy and would call me back when she got to it. I never thought she'd call back. But I couldn't believe it when three weeks later she called. My sisters and I were baptized on January 6, 1956. I was a child of

God, and I didn't even know it. My community had always been there. I
was a prodigal daughter.

Lori took her time. The initial period of inquiry was certainly open-ended in
this congregation, and Lori was consistently reminded that there was no "end
result" compelling her toward affirmation of baptism and/or joining the church.
She, like Maly, took advantage of the invitation to take more time discerning
her participation in this Christian congregation. Newcomers and sponsors vary
along a wide continuum in terms of the vocabulary used to describe faith.
The participants, while in control of what, when, and how they share their
experiences, learn to trust the gathered community as the community meets
together. Lori's questions grew increasingly more complicated as she learned to
trust the process. In turn, Lori was encouraged by her sponsor, the catechist, and
the pastor to enjoy the mystery and promise behind her questions, as opposed to
answering them. What is remarkable about Lori's story is that she continued to
worship in the early years, even as her participation in a constellation of other
central practices in her congregation ebbed and flowed. The practice of worship
was central for her, but it was also supported by a variety of other spaces that
entertained her questions within the community.

DISCIPLESHIP PRACTICES

PARTICIPATING IN WORSHIP

The congregations I researched that practiced intentional newcomer welcome
consistently encouraged participation in the community's primary worship
service. One pastor described his core conviction for the whole congregation
as being to "make regular worship a priority in life." "Worship," he would
reiterate constantly, "is at the heart of your spiritual journey and your
relationship with God and with other church members." When a member
and leading university theologian was not attending worship regularly, this
pastor took him out to lunch and asked him directly why worship was not
a priority for him and his family. For this pastor, all programs, including the
newcomer-welcoming process, flow from and toward the faithful congregation
that gathers around word and sacrament on Sunday morning.

Worship is, for catechumenal congregations, a central practice that
grounds the ministry of welcoming newcomers. As previously noted,
congregational leaders encourage participation in worship as a key marker for
the newcomer's sense of affiliation with the congregation. In nearly all cases,

pastors, catechists, sponsors, and newcomers I interviewed could describe in rich detail why worship was important for the congregation and why worship was essential to nourish the faith given to them by the Holy Spirit. Deeply hidden in the quotes of those interviewed were expressions of "holiness" about the liturgical rites. Worship experiences were "extraordinary" and "powerful." In these churches, worship is participatory, engaging, and inviting and at the same time, something that happens to you through the power of the Holy Spirit.

In congregations that intentionally welcome newcomers, however, worship does not stand alone. Worship is supported by a constellation of other practices. In disestablishment congregations, participation in worship is facilitated because "preparation" for worship is equally important. The meaning of the Easter Vigil, for instance, was shared with participants in the Easter Vigil at a "dress rehearsal" at one congregation. This dress rehearsal took time to help newcomers, sponsors, and catechists know where to stand and practice what to say. But more importantly, this dress rehearsal rehearsed the ancient story of why the night before Easter, in particular, is set apart in the liturgical year to celebrate baptism.

Within the first few minutes I spent at the dress rehearsal, I was caught up in preparing for worship. The biblical text for the evening was Israel crossing the Red Sea in Exodus. The pastor described the Easter Vigil as a liturgical Red Sea and painted a vivid image of Jesus taking us away from our slavery to sin to freedom—from dying to rising. The pastor said, "What lies ahead is a life-changing event, whether you are getting your brows wet [as affirmers] or whether you are leaving your old life behind and taking up a new life [through baptism]. It's not about a single night but a lifetime—every day drowning to sin." Then the pastor shared a Talmudic proverb: "The children of Israel after the crossing of the Red Sea ask God to celebrate and dance. God says, 'My children are drowned, and you expect me to dance?' There is still a dark side, in me, my relationships, in the church, and in the world." He urged the gathering to claim the story and the dark side within ourselves and the larger story to which we belong in community. "Only through community," he exclaimed, "do we live the promise that God has in store for us on the other side of the sea."

At the end of the evening, the pastor reminded participants in The Way to bring to the Easter Vigil a "cup or vessel" representing their vocation in daily life. (That morning, during Palm Sunday worship, the pastor had reminded everyone in the congregation to do the same.) When they arrived for the Easter Vigil, they should leave their cup or vessel on a table in the narthex. During the service of readings, ushers would fill up their vessel with water.

Before the baptismal remembrance, the whole congregation would proceed out of the worship space, using the side aisles, pick up their vessel filled with water, and walk up the center aisle to the large baptismal trough located up a few stairs in the chancel, and pour out the water contained within their vessel, representing their Christian calling in the world, sharing our vocations visibly with those who would be baptized. A week later, as a researcher and participant, I took my paper cup (reserved for visitors) and walked up to the huge trough in the chancel together with three hundred in attendance, pouring my vessel of water into the waters that would baptize two candidates that night. In this congregation, at intentional moments during the Easter Vigil, the whole congregation moves to fill the font with water, to share the peace, to receive Communion, and to be anointed with oil—participating in the central practices of the means of grace and living the promises together as community.

Even as a researcher, I was drawn into the practice, since I not only participated by walking forward with my filled paper cup to pour water into the font but also knew why the act was important and what that act symbolized—or, perhaps more plainly, made real. Here it is necessary to explore a bit more what I mean by "practice." Practice is not only the act of doing something. A practice is also constituted by the meaning that arises from a task situated and shared in a historical and social context. The historical context of the Easter Vigil was made meaningful through the biblical stories shared in the dress rehearsal. The social context was encountered in the gathering of sponsors and newcomers preparing through their own conversation and reflection for the "life-changing event." Participation is not the mere act of doing something. Participation includes negotiating the meaning of central practices, oldcomers and newcomers together. Disestablishment congregations understand that participation means making space for the newcomer's question.

PARTICIPATING IN PUBLIC RITES OF WELCOME

Every congregation I researched used public rites of welcome during its primary worship service to mark different periods of the newcomer-welcoming process. When asked if she remembered any of the public rites in the catechumenate, one college-aged participant responded:

> There were four different times that you have to go in front of the church. I had to go and accept a Bible [during the welcome rite]. I didn't have one, so that was great. The second time, I was given a scroll [of the Apostles' Creed, hand-calligraphed]. I haven't opened it

yet, because it is tied so nicely and I want to buy a frame. The third time was a blessing, and the last time, I got my own hymnal. Each time, there was a blessing to say, and the church would be with me. And then there was my baptism.

In her response, I was struck by how personally she experienced these public rites within worship. I learned that this was not uncommon. The rite of welcome was by far the most memorable rite, commented on by nearly all those interviewed, newcomers and sponsors alike. At the start of the worship service, inquirers and their sponsors stand at the entryway to the sanctuary. Inquirers are presented by their sponsors, asked a few questions, prayed for, and welcomed into the worshipping space. During the worship service, inquirers and their sponsors are invited forward for a blessing. Each sponsor traces the sign of the cross on the inquirer's forehead, ears, eyes, lips, heart, shoulders, hands, and feet. After the blessing, each inquirer receives a Bible. Henry describes it this way:

> We all went up as a part of the service, and we all went up front, and there was a "signing of the cross." Eyes, mouths, shoulders, feet—it was symbolic of the goings on, but it was very, that is, you're taking the whole—it's not just an intellectual Sunday where you should be listening to God, but this is what you should be thinking about: when you speak, be careful what you are saying. It was sort of this outward sign that you were willing to not just say it to yourself, "Let's pray now," but you were willing to stand up in front of the whole church and say, "Fine, yeah, all right, I will do this." It was almost like a smaller precursor to the affirmation of baptism. It was—you were willing to stand up and say, "Here I am," saying, "Count me in."

Another college-aged catechumen recalled the final blessing within the welcome rite, when the whole congregation is invited to extend both hands toward the inquirers:

> I think the one—I think it must have been the first one back in January, I don't know, after New Year's. I went up front, and what was really kind of *whoa* was when everyone puts their hands up. Everyone is focusing on me. It's really welcoming to think about. I don't know how to put it, but they are focusing on you, and soon I'm going to be a part of the congregation, and I'll be able to focus on somebody else.

A lifelong Lutheran and member of her congregation since she was a child agreed to be a sponsor for a baptismal candidate. She gets to the heart of the matter with this description:

> There were people who asked me why I did it. It was my own choice, and I saw it as an opportunity to be a part of what was happening here, rather than just seeing people go up and being a part of the different blessings. Some of those blessings were very touching moments.

The one I remember in particular is the blessing with all the parts of your body. From an observer's point of view it's kind of "What are they doing now? Why are they doing the feet?" But to be a part of it—I can say that I was a part of that, and it was very impressive. I've grown from that.

> There is something about going up close to the altar and having these things occur which is different when you sit in the pew. To have the whole group there [pause]. One thing that I am saying is, if you don't participate in something like this as a sponsor, it's really hard to explain to people. It's just something that comes from your heart. That participation is the most vivid thing I remember. So every year when I hear that music, and I could sing it for you, it inspires me to be a part of it again. If you experience something, the wounded healer understands, and otherwise . . . , sometimes . . . , you just can't get it.

The experience of participating in the rites, as described here, speaks not only to the centrality of worship but also to the importance of participation and the personal nature of the extended promise.

PARTICIPATING IN BIBLE STUDY AND PRAYER

Conversion and discernment of God's call take time and cannot be rushed, so in the congregations I researched, emphasis is placed on regular and consistent Bible study and prayer prior to baptism or joining a congregation. In the resources introducing the catechumenate, a gradual catechesis for the adult newcomer is modeled upon the rite of welcome. In this rite, admittedly the most significant among the public rites of the catechumenate as described above, the sponsor traces the sign of the cross upon the newcomer, moving from forehead to ears, eyes, lips, heart, shoulders, hands, and feet. "It is a gesture of evangelization: the entire person—body, mind, and spirit—is claimed for Christ."[18] The forehead symbolizes the newcomer's questioning faith and the honest dialogue that takes place within catechesis, as opposed to formulated answers provided by the catechist. Newcomers are encouraged to hear the Scriptures with their ears, exploring the Bible in Christian community and learning how to pray for the needs of one another. Each newcomer has the opportunity to watch other Christians with his or her eyes: "Sponsors and mentors may provide 'testimonials' of how they live the faith in their daily lives."[19] Newcomers are encouraged to speak the faith with their lips, participating together with the congregation's liturgy, in prayer, and within the public realm of daily life for the cause of justice and peace. The newcomer's heart symbolizes the equal regard the catechumenate gives to "knowledge of the faith" and the slow, holistic transformation that negotiating life as a Christian disciple encourages within the person. Receiving the sign of the cross upon his or her shoulders, hands, and feet supports the newcomer's daily work and walk that define the Christian vocation of service to neighbor and the world.

Nearly all of the congregations gather inquirers and their sponsors biweekly from October through December and then weekly from January through Easter and throughout the days of Pentecost. The catechumenate gatherings include opportunities for God's word to engage the participant's whole life—body, mind, and spirit—and reflection upon God's calling in the participant's life. Catechists, sponsors, and newcomers—all are encouraged to use their primary language of faith as they reflect upon the text, using firsthand experiences and stories, as opposed to talking *about* faith.

Six of the eight congregations consistently practice what the ELCA resources call the African Bible Study or *Collatio* during those biweekly or weekly gatherings.[20] This study, used in base Christian communities in South Africa, encourages participants to listen to the text that is read aloud and respond. "This method turns Bible study away from the intellectual pursuit of knowledge about the text and toward an attitude of listening to what God is saying through the text."[21]

The newcomer-welcoming process in these congregations begins with prayer and the reading of the Gospel appointed for Sunday of that week.[22] After a period of silence, individuals are invited to share a word, phrase, or image from the text that catches their attention and speaks to their life at this time.[23] The passage is read a second time, and silence is kept again. During the second sharing, participants are invited to talk about how the text is speaking to them directly or to their relationships with others. After a third reading and a third period of silence, the final invitation is to speak the prayer that grows out of the text and reflect on it.[24] In some groups, the sponsor and the newcomer pray for one another before the gathering closes with those prayers arising from the text and a hymn.

A cruciform catechesis involves conversation among peers, newcomers, and oldcomers together. Although the catechist is present to facilitate the gathering, he or she is not the authority or knowledge bearer in the room. Catechists, sponsors, and inquirers alike share authority and knowledge. Any residual authority the catechist has early in the process is transferred to the biblical text that is read aloud and to the stories and experiences shared by the participants. Further, the African Bible Study does not presume a knowledge base from the participant other than that which the participants offer through their experience. For newcomers who have not been baptized or those seeking to affirm their baptism, this Bible study method creates a nonthreatening, safe atmosphere for adults to explore what they do not know or understand about the faith. This atmosphere is particularly crucial for sponsors, who speak of the process as a "renewing" or a "refreshing" of their faith. Sponsors often said, "I certainly got more out of the catechumenate, perhaps more than the person I was sponsoring," or, "It was just as much for me as it was for her."

The African Bible Study follows a consistent pattern that participants come to trust as the weeks pass. This pattern elicits memories and fosters connections between the Scripture text and daily life, which are then shared among group members from week to week. As individuals described their experience with the African Bible Study, they used terms such as "multiple voices," "deeper meanings," "ambiguity," and "meaningful to my life." The study consistently revealed that everyone held different perspectives of the biblical text and that the text elicited a variety of stories. Henry noted:

> That's been the really amazing thing about what other people will pull out. I didn't even hear—wow—it's just—I know that, like, just last week when I got together just for our one-on-one,[25] the question he came up with was just a hundred and eighty degrees away from mine. And then our answers: It was just, well, "What is the color of the sky?" Well it's everything, or it's blue or green or purple. So that's really nice.
>
> I no longer really look at the Gospel or the sermons with quite the face value that I once did. It's a part of that seeing it in a group, so it's like, oh! So I will go home and read the Gospel and think at a whole other level, you know, deeper and further in. They parted the sea, they went through—okay, fine, but what does that mean?

You know, it's not just at face value; there is a lot more to it. And oftentimes, it's like something completely different than what you initially heard in the service.

I also think about Pastor when he does his sermon. *[Whistles.]* He just roars into them, and then, bam!, turns the corner and shows you the other side of it. It's like "Oh, whoa!" He kind of leads you into it, and then, bang!, this is what he meant by this, and not what you were really thinking. Between those two [the gatherings and the sermons], it has really struck home. I think the way it was written in the old language and tried to translate it into today—they are written, the stories are written at different levels. That has been lifted up for me.

The African Bible Study equips newcomers and oldcomers with a way to read scripture faithfully in community. The regular sharing and reflecting on the biblical text that occur in this method teach a hermeneutic for interpreting the text in light of the whole community's encounter with God. Participants gain a new appreciation for the variety of interpretations that exist around any one text. As Henry engaged in catechesis and prayer through the deliberate process of newcomer welcome, Henry also learned to appreciate the pastor's sermons in meaningful ways. What is equally remarkable about Lori's story is the way she describes herself in terms of the biblical characters. Throughout our conversation, she referred to Adam or Thomas or her favorite, the woman at the well, embodying their voices as she quoted scripture and wove these characters into her own story.

PARTICIPATING IN PERIPHERAL PRACTICES

Catechumenate practitioners place a priority on worship, Bible study, and prayer and facilitate newcomer participation in those Christian practices central to the communal, sacramental life of the congregation. These, however, are not the only practices to be facilitated. Peripheral practices of hospitality, outreach, mutual care for others, and advocacy were often explored by newcomers as part of the welcoming process.

A video that accompanies the resources introducing the catechumenate process to ELCA congregations tells the story of a young man seeking baptism at a Lutheran church in the Northwest. A critical component of the catechumenate process in that congregation is the time this young man spends accompanying his sponsor to a soup kitchen to serve meals. In addition to serving, these two spend time getting to know those who come to eat. The sponsor of this young man models this faithful Christian practice and meaningfully articulates such actions as serving a neighbor, hospitality to the stranger, walking with the poor, and more. One sponsor I interviewed told me she spends nearly every waking hour volunteering in the hospital, visiting and praying with patients. Henry, of course, served food for the congregational meals and volunteered at the food bank located in the church.

Sometimes peripheral practices are the unique, local ones that only oldcomers in this congregation know to do. And sometimes peripheral practices erupt in a moment in time and quickly become integrated into the narrative of the congregation's life. For instance, one new member shared with me her story about how she singlehandedly persuaded the congregation at a congregational meeting to host the homeless on their front lawn for a week. As a brand-new member, she stood up and spoke eloquently about the ministry of service to which she had been called as a Christian in her baptism. She told the attendees that she had no intention of staying connected to a congregation that refused to help those in need. She was effective. The congregation voted yes.

A newcomer's presence in a congregation as a liminal, not quite sure whether they are included in "my people," is unsettling. Newcomers exemplify the fluidity that characterizes contemporary American religious identity and heighten the oldcomer's experience of hybridity in relation to Christian discipleship and Christian identity. Participating together in central and peripheral practices, newcomers and oldcomers alike take on the task of negotiating what Christian discipleship looks like, entertaining the ultimate question, "who are my people?"

And more, newcomers embody God's promise in their questions, even as the questions inevitably give rise to more questions among oldcomers. God's logic in all this is foolishness. This is *our* God who turns reason and experience on their heads, *our* God who demands particularity and exclusivity on the one hand and simultaneously demands unabashed love and inclusivity on the other, thus acting in surprising and unexpected ways. "For as the heavens are higher than the earth, so are my ways higher than your ways and my thoughts than your thoughts" (Isa. 55:9). God's promise is extended. God's promise is on the move. Thus, at the boundary of the church and the world, the *solas* and the *simuls*, newcomers and oldcomers together negotiate their identity as Christians. When I experienced Maly's questions as my own, I was driven toward a renewed sense of Christian identity and eagerness to figure out what my church understood as faithfulness. Maly's faithfulness in pursuing the questions invited me to explore Christian identity at the boundary between the world and the church—literally on the street outside the church. In the presence of Maly and her question, I glimpsed the promise of God's presence. For a moment, I imagined a bigger vision of the promise, wondering how that promise she and I both longed for might become realized.

Notes

1. Robert Putnam and David Campbell, *American Grace: How Religion Unites and Divides Us* (New York: Simon and Schuster, 2010), 136.

2. Ibid., 135–36.

3. Ibid., 136.

4. Ibid., 135.

5. The covenant formula is found in the context of the Priestly Pentateuch, in Deuteronomy, and the prophets. Rolf Rendtorff, *The Covenant Formula: An Exegetical and Theological Investigation*, trans. Margaret Kohl, Old Testament Studies, ed. David J. Reimer, (Edinburgh: T & T Clark, 1998).

6. Leviticus also recalls the promise: "And I will walk among you, and will be your God and you will be my people" (Lev. 26:12).

7. Donald E. Gowan, "Amos," in *The New Interpreter's Bible*, ed. Leander Keck (Nashville: Abingdon, 1996), 423.

8. See Peter Cruchley-Jones, "Entering Exile: Can There Be a Missiology for 'Not My People'?," in *A Scandalous Prophet: The Way of Mission after Newbigin*, ed. Thomas F. Foust, George R. Hunsburger, J. Andrew Kirk, and Werner Ustorf (Grand Rapids: Eerdmans, 2002), 28.

9. Gowan cautions against overreading Amos here: "It would be moving far beyond anything this text could support to say that Amos was a 'universalist' that he believed each nation had its means of access to the true God. . . . But by making this claim for the universal sovereignty of Yahweh, Amos marks the beginning of serious consideration, by the prophets, of the nations as something more than enemies." Gowan, "Amos," 425.

10. Cruchley-Jones, "Entering Exile," 29.

11. This is J. Clinton McCann's translation of this verse. J. Clinton McCann, "Commentary on Hosea 1:2–10," *Working Preacher.org* (Luther Seminary), July 25, 2010, http://www.workingpreacher.org/preaching.aspx?lect_date=7/25/2010&tab=2.

12. Sarah Henrich, "Oh, the Honesty of Thomas and Philip," *Working Preacher.org* (Luther Seminary), May 22, 2011, http://www.workingpreacher.org/preaching.aspx?lect_date=5/22/2011&tab=4.

13. J. Paul Rajashekar, "Navigating Difficult Questions," in *The Evangelizing Church: A Lutheran Contribution*, ed. Richard H. Bliese and Craig Van Gelder (Minneapolis: Augsburg Fortress, 2005), 98.

14. Ibid., 99.

15. Ibid., 101.

16. Martin E. Marty, "Articles of War, Articles of Peace: Christianity and Culture," in *Christ and Culture in Dialogue: Constructive Themes and Practical Applications*, ed. Angus J. L. Menuge (St. Louis: Concordia Academic, 1999), 60.

17. Kathryn Tanner, *Theories of Culture: A New Agenda for Theology*, Guides to Theological Inquiry (Minneapolis: Fortress Press, 1997), 101.

18. Samuel Torvend and Lani Willis, eds., *Welcome to Christ: A Lutheran Catechetical Guide* (Minneapolis: Augsburg Fortress, 1997), 12–13.

19. Ibid., 10.

20. A second method for catechesis is suggested in the ELCA resources: encouraging catechumens to visualize the text through drama or art. This method was not used by any of the congregations studied. Ibid., 49.

21. Ibid.

22. Some congregations read the text from the previous Sunday, others for the upcoming Sunday.

23. Torvend and Willis, *Welcome to Christ*, 49.

24. Ibid., 50.

25. One-on-one time is an opportunity within the gatherings for the sponsor and the candidate to share apart from the group, alone with one another.

3

Facilitating Newcomer Participation

Facilitating participation involves cultivating trust between newcomers and oldcomers and exploring knowledge and skill again and again when disarticulation occurs within discipleship practices. Attending to trust and competence leads newcomers to experience a sense of belonging to a particular community. For oldcomers, participating in discipleship practices with newcomers offers a renewed sense of belonging to their particular community as it evolves through a cruciform catechesis.

Social Learning Theory

By describing learning as occurring between newcomers and oldcomers and not within an individual mind, I am talking about a social theory of learning. In contrast, learning is often understood through cognitive theories, which emphasize memory and the prior experience necessary for the brain to process more information. A newcomer's class framed within a cognitive learning theory tells newcomers what they need to know and may ask questions about prior experiences to help the participants frame new knowledge about the community. Learning studies have proven, however, that what you know does not necessarily lead to a change in how you behave. Social learning theories seek to explore how learning occurs between people through observation, participation, and motivation and how these elements together lead to a change in behavior. A social learning theory also recognizes that learning mediates the different perspectives held within a community.[1] In other words, all participants contribute through their differences of opinion to the learning that occurs within the community, including oldcomers and newcomers alike. Ultimately, learning that facilitates participation by negotiating difference meaningfully leads to trust, competence, and belonging in a community.[2]

Etienne Wenger's work as a researcher of human learning began as a joint project with Jean Lave that investigated apprenticeship models of education. Wenger and Lave's research into specific historical instances of apprenticeship led to the recognition that the "master" in the master/apprentice learning design was not the metaphorical expert passing on valuable information to the unknowledgeable apprentice, as a cognitive learning theory might describe.[3] Much more is going on in this relationship. Apprenticeship learning is fully situated within a complex social practice emphasizing and involving the whole person, rather than simply "receiving" a body of factual knowledge about the world.[4] Designing a theory of social learning for congregations provides a stronger way to approach catechesis occurring within the newcomer-welcoming processes. A disestablished church recognizes that discipleship is learned and newcomers need to learn how to participate in communities of disciples.[5]

Wenger explores the concepts of community and practice as they lead to an individual's development of an identity in relation to the community and an individual's sense of belonging to the community. At the heart of these concepts is the place of participation, mutuality, and negotiation between the individual and the community. Prior to this chapter, I refrained from using the word *community*, because I wanted to define that word very specifically. I am not using this term *community* as it is often used referring to a location, neighbors, friends, or like interests. Communities are described by what they do, by who is involved in the task, and by what that task means to participants. Community is defined by practice; practice happens in community.[6] Communities of practice, then, involve the mutual engagement of participants in a joint task over time that creates resources for negotiating meaning, constructing individual and corporate identity, and producing knowledge.[7]

Congregations are made up of multiple communities of practice. Each community within a congregation has a task or multiple tasks of discipleship around which they gather. Altar guilds care for holy things in relation to the community's practice of worship and sacraments. Trustees care for the physical property that serves the community's ministry in relation to the practice of stewardship. To participate in these communities, newcomers need access to these resources and meanings to enable their participation in the community. Without deliberately designed access, newcomers will feel marginalized—the opposite of participation. Access is what translates into trust.

COMMUNITIES AND PRACTICE

PARTICIPATION AND IDENTITY

When either belonging or involvement is missing, participation is partial. A newcomer can be a member of an organization through a public rite after a few classes with the pastor but not invited into the discipleship tasks that the congregation undertakes. Or a newcomer can be involved in a discipleship task but not actually belong through membership. (I am thinking about the choir member who is involved weekly in the congregation's worship but does not belong to the congregation, or about the child who attends Sunday school every week but whose parent sits in the car.) A newcomer who is involved in an activity at the congregation but does not belong does not have the same kind of emotional investment as a member who is involved in a meaningful way. Or vice versa: a member of the congregation might not be involved in anything and thus be only a participant as a name on the congregational roster. Participation "is a complex process that combines doing, talking, thinking, feeling, and belonging. It involves our whole person, including our bodies, minds, emotions, and social relations."[8]

Participation without belonging or involvement is sometimes the experience of nonparticipation. Nonparticipation has two forms. First, marginality occurs when boundaries are unattended, ignored, or undesignated. If a newcomer experiences marginality, he might decide not to belong or not to become involved. "Everybody is welcome" is a significant slogan on a church sign or for a mission statement, but often it is also evidence of an ignored boundary. Congregations desire to remove or ignore boundaries, seeking to reduce the tension, rushing membership, and ignoring newcomer questions in the process. The boundary of a practice is where newcomers ask questions. Nonparticipation can be the very particular boundary of a practice that cries out for interpretation. Disestablished congregations can identify what discipleship practices might elicit the experience of nonparticipation among newcomers and describe the boundary. This second form of nonparticipation is peripherality, the opposite of marginality.[9] I will return to this concept of peripherality later in this chapter. Naming what conversations, resources, and histories the newcomer may not initially understand is a start to identifying the boundary. Access to these elements of a practice is crucial for nonparticipation to lead to participation.

Newcomers do not expect to be full participants in an organization right away. They encounter the boundary of nonparticipation and need oldcomers to explore the boundary with them. The work of exploration and interpretation at the boundaries risks change, and that change can result in a disestablished congregation recognizing that it has to die to some of its old ways of doing things and be born anew by the participation of newcomers. This is the entropic principle of the *ecclesia crucis*. The community of practice is never the same when mutual learning takes place within the *ecclesia crucis*.

Participation implies not only belonging and involvement but also mutual recognition. Newcomers who encounter participation as marginality will not feel as though they are recognized for who they are as human beings and what they have to offer the community. Nonparticipation, whether marginality or peripherality, becomes as much a part of our identity as participation. Newcomers who experience recognition also experience an affirmation of their identity. This experience of mutual recognition encourages participation and is the source of identity definition. That another recognizes me is the impetus for me to discover for myself who I am becoming.[10]

Oldcomers within congregations do identify with the communities of practice in which they are involved. As an associate pastor, I once was called in to mediate confusion within the altar guild. The chair of the altar guild was stepping down, and a new person was taking over the position. A question arose over how many purificators should be placed on the altar for communion. In the past, three had been placed, although there were only two chalices. When the new chair asked the old chair why there were three purificators when only two were needed, the response was that the three purificators represented the Trinity. This was not just a glib matter, and the old chair had a stake in the theological conviction that the Trinity be represented through the purificators during the sacrament of Holy Communion. This was meaningful to her and therefore also deeply meaningful to her identity as the altar guild chair, whose responsibility it is to care for holy things. Her identity as altar guild chair also translated into how she viewed herself as a participant in the congregation as a whole. She made possible through her coordination and training of volunteers on the altar guild the congregation's experience of worship and particularly the sacrament of Holy Communion. Although the new altar guild chair did not continue the practice of placing three purificators on the table, she learned through this interaction with her mentor more about her identity as the new altar guild chair. She, too, is to care for holy things in a way that matters theologically and practically, while also managing the coordination and training of volunteers and facilitating the congregation's worship experience. Note the elements worked out within this brief encounter. What some might see as a conflict interpreted through language of nonparticipation and participation is clearly an opportunity for the community of disciples to negotiate meaning around their task and, through this mutual engagement, also discern their identity as Christian disciples. Participation together with peripheral access shapes identity and belonging within communities of practice.

It is through identities of participation that we learn. Yet Wenger insists also that by learning, we "acquire an identity of participation."[11] This is the paradox of learning. The way into and beyond the paradox is through mutuality:

> In the life-giving power of mutuality lies the miracle of parenthood, the essence of apprenticeship, the secret to the generational encounter, the key to the creation of connections across boundaries of practice: a frail bridge across the abyss, a slight breach of the law, a small gift of undeserved trust—it is almost a *theorem of love* that we can open our practices and communities to others (newcomers, outsiders), invite them into our own identities of participation, let them be what they are not, and thus start what cannot be started.[12]

Ultimately, Wenger does not have the resources within his social theory of learning to investigate this theorem of love, this learning about ourselves in deep mutuality with another that is motivated by openness and love toward the other. Thinking theologically, however, we can identify the acquisition of identity through our identity of participation—within parenthood, apprenticeship, generational encounter, or even newcomer-welcoming processes between oldcomers and newcomers—as the means of grace made evident through the mutual care among brothers and sisters. It is not "almost a theorem of love" that motivates oldcomers to open practices to the peripheral participation of newcomers. It *is* a theorem of love. Love becomes tangible as newcomers appear at the threshold of congregations, weary, broken, and worn, searching for meaning, purpose, identity, and new life. Love is the compulsion to welcome these newcomers, eager to hear their questions, encountering God's promises, and transforming the congregation's orientation toward God to the world. It is a love that compels a cruciform identity—one that dies so that others might live.

REIFICATION AND IDENTITY

Together with participation, Wenger sets forth yet another concept that is critical for communities of practice. The constitutive duality of participation is the community's natural propensity toward *reification*. Reification is not embodied as participation is; it is abstract, a projection—the formulation of the community's practice through tools, symbols, stories, terms, concepts, documents, forms, etc. Neither participation nor reification is ever complete in and of itself, but both are essential to a community's existence. Yet as with nonparticipation, which can potentially lead to marginality instead of peripherality, the reified forms of a community's practice can also be misunderstood. Reifications have historic and present meanings within a community that can hide a community's deliberations and struggle over a matter. Or reification can become a monument that is detached from the participants of a community—an object without meaning. Still, reification is indispensable: "Reification is essential to repairing the potential misalignments inherent in participation: when the informality of participation is confusingly loose, when the fluidity of its implicitness impedes coordination, when its locality is too confining or its partiality too narrow, then it is reification that comes to the rescue."[13]

Participation and reification are critical to the learning process in communities of practice, as they are the source for remembering and forgetting. Apart from the ability to participate in a community of practice, individuals do not have memories. Apart from the ability to reify its practice, a community does not have a history. The interplay of participation and reification establishes the ground for mutual recognition and negotiation of meaning between newcomers and oldcomers of a community.

Within newcomer-welcoming processes, the shared historical resources of a practice include the oldcomers' memories and collective congregational history in addition to the biblical text within a broadly conceived "deposit of faith" including the creeds, confessions, liturgies, catechisms, and disciplines of faith, to name a few. The social resources might consist of the present activity of the oldcomers in addition to the congregation's denominational identity, social location, and physical location. These shared historical and social resources are passed along through dynamic participation frameworks such as the communities of practice that gather newcomers and oldcomers together regularly for biblical engagement, prayer, worship, care for one another, and service toward neighbor. The shared historical and social resources become meaningful over time as the different perspectives of oldcomers are encountered in discipleship practices and meaning is negotiated. Practice, defined in this way, is not innate or instinctual; rather, it "requires some catching up for joining."[14] Practices are learned through participation in communities.

To identify the dynamics of participation and reification, perhaps an exaggerated example is in order. In many congregations, the kitchen is a contentious location within the church building. Written and unwritten rules guide who can and who cannot use the kitchen. The individuals who make the rules are the participants who take their ministry so seriously that the kitchen and their participation in what it represents within the congregation become an investment of their sense of belonging to the community of practice that works in the kitchen and in turn their identity in relationship to the congregation. The very fact that rules need to be made with regard to the kitchen indicates the tenuous, messy, and perhaps unstable reality of practice in community. Reification is needed to enable the participation of all who need to use a common space. Yet over time, reification may take on a life of its own apart from the situated context and may lead to misunderstandings and rigid attitudes and postures. This is a common experience within communities of practice. Newcomers often encounter reified forms of a practice and wonder about the origin. While reification is necessary, the duality of reification together with participation is what keeps a community's practice vital and vibrant.

Catechists and pastors can use the language of participation and nonparticipation (both peripheral and marginal) and reification (as both memory and history, remembered and forgotten) to encourage the negotiations between oldcomers and newcomers within newcomer-welcoming processes. Additionally, catechisms and other theological understandings can be used not with the fear of indoctrination that might come from a cognitive learning theory, but with the honest need for newcomers to explore the reified stories, symbols, practices, concepts, documents, and forms of the community's practice. Every reified source has a history to tell of its development through a community of practice. Sometimes describing such developments is just what is needed for catching up and learning a practice. Other times, the history becomes the gateway to whole new understandings and interpretations. Without these reified forms of nonparticipation, newcomers would not have to learn how to participate within the community of practice. Without reified resources of faith, belief could be anything. Here the *solas* in the scandal of their particularity announce their presence within the community and call out to be engaged by both newcomers and oldcomers.

As we have been exploring so far, the presence of newcomers within a community of practice is what encourages the viability of practices. Although a practice is never the same from week to week or moment to moment, because the situated time and space are different, the generational encounter of newcomers and oldcomers does expose the need for review and exploration of any practice within a community. To explore this vibrant process of keeping a practice alive, we will now consider in detail the three constituent parts of Wenger's notion of a community of practice.

COMMUNITIES OF PRACTICE

Learning is an experience of meaning interacting with a process of developing competence. The focal point for what defines a community is how Wenger's concept of practice interacts with the three dimensions in his definition of community: (1) mutual engagement, (2) a joint enterprise, and (3) a shared repertoire. These three dimensions enable and encourage participation in an experience of meaning that over time leads to the development of competence, identity, and a sense of belonging.

MUTUAL ENGAGEMENT

Wenger uses practice at the level of discourse, defining practice by virtue of the meanings which arise from sustained *mutual engagement* among people.[15] Within a community of practice, this mutual engagement happens face-to-face. The African Bible Study enables newcomers and oldcomers participating in catechumenate communities of practice to create a web of meaning around a lectionary pericope. This meaning arises from the negotiated perceptions of the individuals involved. The text and its interpretation are not owned by a particular knowledge bearer, but rather belong to the community of practice. Individuals reflecting on the pericope text in light of their own experiences learn to trust the community and the process over time, mutually recognizing the importance of everyone's contribution as necessary for the creation of meaning. This community of practice is the participatory framework in which meaning—the text's interpretation—is embedded.

Routines sustain a community's practice through mutual engagement. Henry identified how the sustained weekly meetings of the catechumenate group became routine. Meaning arising from routine engagement is not limited to language but includes the affective, the senses, and the physical body. The routine participation framework is not just the perception of others; it includes embodied others. For Henry, the community gathered for dinner and biblical study became a meaning-filled place to share *ourselves*—"our whole selves, not only our faith."

Although practice is routine, it is simultaneously dynamic. The way of talking about the shared lectionary text is never the same from year to year, from week to week, or from group to group. The unique experiences of individuals present and the partial knowledge each brings to the shared meanings and interpretations create an inimitable practice. Just as sand castles are created and then washed away, even routine activities begin and end anew each time. Wenger writes,

> When we sit down for lunch for the thousandth time with the same colleagues in the same cafeteria, we have seen it all before. We know all the steps. We may even know today's menu by heart; we may love it or we may dread it. And yet we eat again, we taste again. We may know our colleagues very well, and yet we repeatedly engage in conversation. All that we do and say may refer to what has been done and said in the past, and yet we produce again a new situation, an impression, and experience: we produce meanings that extend, redirect, dismiss, reinterpret, modify or confirm—in a word, negotiate anew—the histories of meanings of which they are part. In a sense, living is a constant process of negotiation of meaning.[16]

Wenger contends (as does Tanner) that meaning exists in the process of negotiation; it is not owned by individuals. "Meaning exists neither in us, nor in the world, but in the dynamic relation of living in the world."[17] To make meaning is to live deeply in mutual engagement as humans together in the world.

To make meaning because of being mutually engaged in a face-to-face encounter within a community of practice is to be a member. This warrants repeating when it comes to congregations and communities of practice. To be a member of a community of practice is to be mutually engaged in the meaning-making process. Let me be clear, congregations are not to be equated with communities of practice. Congregations are made up of multiple communities of practice. For instance, the newcomer-welcoming group involving catechists, sponsors, newcomers, and pastors as participants engaged in a meaning-making process around a joint enterprise is just one community of practice. Multiple communities of practice exist within the congregation; the choir, the youth group, the ushers, the Sunday school teachers and classes, small groups, the acolytes, the women's circle, and the finance committee might all be considered communities of practice. Furthermore, membership in a community of practice does not preclude an individual from having multiple memberships. Individuals are participants in numerous communities of practice each and every day. Individuals can and do hold multiple memberships within one organization.

Some congregations are communities by virtue of their size. Wenger has noted that communities will divide into subgroups after they number about fifty people. Beyond fifty, subcommunities naturally develop around topics and geographical location, and lead to the development of strong local identities. "These nested subcommunities within a single large community allow members to be very engaged locally while retaining a sense of belonging to the larger community."[18] Thus, subcommunities keep constituents engaged with a larger community. Congregations that worship below fifty on average might be considered communities of practice in and of themselves. However, gathering to experience an event, such as worship, is not the only criterion that defines a community. As is clear by the definition, communities of practice facilitate and enable interactions among those involved. These interactions establish the practice.[19]

Congregations are organizations made up of various and smaller communities of practice and are themselves valuable communities of practice in relation to the wider web of congregations and volunteer organizations in the United States.[20] To maintain their effectiveness and value in a social setting in which people's transient nature is a given (newcomers arrive, members die or move), the boundaries of congregations are porous (ecumenical conversations have led to large shifts in membership among denominations), and cultural expectations still encourage people to seek out communities of faith when in crisis or during important milestones (baptisms, weddings, funerals). Thus, congregations need systematic language for how they function as learning communities to welcome newcomers into their midst.[21] In the next chapter, I will identify how multiple communities of practice exist within the same congregation and how relationships are fostered between each community, but for now, I want to continue exploring communities of practice.

Communities of practice are shared histories of learning. Thus, newcomer learning in practice involves the "evolving forms of *mutual engagement*: discovering how to engage, what helps and what hinders; developing mutual relationships; defining identities; establishing who is who, who is good at what, who knows what, who is easy or hard to get along with."[22] Learning defined in this way involves taking time and opportunities to meet face-to-face for mutual conversation and care. By designing an opportunity to learn through mutual engagement, deliberative newcomer-welcoming processes provide such a time and place.

Joint Enterprise

Wenger's notion of the joint enterprise as the second identifying mark of the community of practice is inherently related to the concept of mutual engagement.[23] The enterprise is a task awaiting discovery. In the catechumenate process, newcomers together with oldcomers engage in a joint enterprise. Engaging the biblical text, exploring meaning in worship and the sacraments, praying for one another, discerning God's call, practicing hospitality, and serving at a soup kitchen are all tasks a newcomer-welcoming group might take up as its joint enterprise. What this joint enterprise looks like varies from group to group from year to year, because the individuals involved negotiate the task.

When individuals are involved in negotiating the enterprise, the enterprise itself becomes deeply personal. Certainly at the more personal level, negotiation does not always entail agreement. Wenger writes, "The enterprise is joint not in that everybody believes the same thing or agrees with everything, but in that it is communally negotiated."[24] Indeed, diversity and partiality are valued in communities of practice. Newcomers in the catechumenate spoke about the value of multiple and different perspectives that arose through the African Bible Study. Together, these multiple perspectives added to the community's overall experience of the biblical text. In fact, mutual engagement is possible only because people value different matters and ideas. If one knew everything about a task or could work alone, a community would not be needed.

In the context of shared learning, partiality is respected: "Because they belong to a community of practice where people help each other, it is more important to know how to give and receive help than to try to know everything yourself."[25] This partiality creates "a regime of mutual accountability."[26] Members of a community show up and do their part because their competence is expected as an important contribution to the joint enterprise. Over time, the joint enterprise itself becomes invested with meanings and histories, establishing accountability among the participants and ultimately informing their identity.

Communities of practice create space for newcomers by acknowledging the partiality of knowledge. Value is given to all perspectives, because at the heart of the community is the perception that knowledge is shared and situated. Knowledge does not exist in the individual mind but rather in the negotiated space within a community of practice. Hence, "our competence gains its value through its very partiality."[27] As I need someone else to complement my partial knowledge, so too is my knowledge necessary within the community of practice. This is the confession of incompleteness that congregations practicing disestablishment must make when the newcomer is not present. And in this confession, the newcomer is welcomed for the knowledge and identity he or she brings to the community of practice. The newcomer's partial knowledge leads to the development of her identity, shaped through participation in a community of practice. The newcomer becomes essential to the community as her experience of meaning within the community becomes valued. Over the course of time, the community recognizes her contribution of meaning and in turn affirms her competence.

Communities of practice are shared histories of learning. Thus, newcomer learning in practice involves defining and understanding the task, participating in the task, engaging in mutual accountability, and reconciling conflicting interpretations of the task.[28] This in turn creates a shared sense of ownership and belonging among participants in the community of practice, which over time leads the participants to value their own competence. Deliberatively designed processes for newcomer welcome provide the structure for newcomers and oldcomers to learn through joint enterprise.

SHARED REPERTOIRE

Over time, communities of practice develop a *shared repertoire*—resources for the ongoing task. "The repertoire of a community of practice includes routines, words, tools, ways of doing things, stories, gestures, symbols, genres, actions, or concepts that the community has produced or adopted in the course of its existence, and which have become part of its practice."[29] This repertoire becomes the histories shared and negotiated over time by the community of practice. Repertoire arises from mutual engagement around a joint enterprise, but it is not always directly related to the joint enterprise. Repertoire might consist of the preliminaries of a conversation: "How are the kids?" or "Have you found a car you like?" One might also include the inside jokes and the colloquialisms used by a community of practice.

Oldcomers of a community are the most valuable resource for newcomers. Congregations are one of the few institutions in which multiple generations gather together to engage in practice with regularity. Organizations that lose sight of the importance of a generational encounter lose sight of their purpose and their future. Wenger writes:

> There are all sorts of reasons to shelter newcomers from the intensity of actual practice, from the power struggles of full participation and possibly from the abuses of established members. Similarly, there

are all sorts of reasons to shelter old-timers from the naiveté of newcomers and spare them the time and trouble of going over the basics. . . . The generational encounter involves not the mere transmission of a cultural heritage, but the mutual negotiation of identities invested in different historical moments. When old-timers and newcomers are engaged in separate practices, they lose the benefit of their interaction.[30]

It is no wonder to me that all the catechumenate congregations in my research have one worship service (or one type of worship service if there is more than one on Sunday) for all generations. Their commitment to the encounter between newcomers and oldcomers has opened the space for mutual engagement around a shared resource, Sunday worship. For far too long, congregations have attempted to market their worship experiences to separate generations. Seeker services aiming to attract newcomers were developed in most cases in spite of the established membership, who worshiped "traditionally." The segregation that resulted has left our communities no better off, no larger, and severely impoverished. In a critically important paragraph about this segregation, Wenger contends:

> In terms of identity, this segregation creates a vacuum. Generational
> issues of identification and negotiability become resolved in isolation.
> Local ownership of meaning is not exposed to broader economies.
> Identification finds material in relationships among newcomers; that
> is, newcomers are having to invent identities and meanings among
> themselves. In this context they can try some pretty wild things,
> but their attempts remain local, self-contained, and without much
> effort on history. Without mutual engagement and accountability
> across generations, new identities can be both erratically inventive
> and historically ineffective.[31]

Oldcomers may also carry with them the shared histories and resources developed from the mutual negotiation of earlier generations. Designing learning in congregations involves deciding what repertoire to use and what repertoire to reject. For example, Luther's Small and Large Catechisms are repertoire developed as the result of a long process of discernment among Martin Luther, Philipp Melanchthon, and local pastors about what was needed by households and pastors to encourage catechesis. Since the sixteenth century, catechisms have been used or rejected as repertoire in Lutheran congregations. Although the use of the catechisms is encouraged in all of the ELCA resources for the catechumenate, catechumenate trainings have reinforced the critique of catechisms as indoctrination so frequently that practitioners disregard the literature's recommendations and do not use the catechisms or other confessional documents of earlier eras. But to recall and tell the historical story of how these documents arose can provide guidance and resource discernment in the present.

Communities of practice are shared histories of learning among newcomers and oldcomers. Thus, learning in practice also involves "developing a community's *repertoire*, styles and discourses: renegotiating the meaning of various elements; producing or adopting tools, artifacts, representations; recording and recalling events; inventing new terms and redefining or abandoning old ones; telling and retelling stories; creating and breaking routines."[32] By designing an opportunity to learn through repertoire, newcomer-welcoming processes provide continuity with the past within the present.

It is vitally important to note here that, contrary to popular notions, newcomers may not want to reject the old or what Wenger calls accentuating discontinuity.[33] Investing in the histories, shared repertoire, and joint enterprise inspires a deep and developing connection that is needed and expected for the formation of identity. Conversely, oldcomers have been around for quite some time and may not want to accentuate continuity. Rather, they may want to break from the past and welcome new and fresh ideas from newcomers that inform and shape their identity in preparation for the future. Generational encounters, although inevitable and necessary, do not always play out in ways we might expect.

DEVELOPING COMPETENCE:
A NEWCOMER'S LEGITIMATE PERIPHERAL PARTICIPATION

To reiterate, learning is an experience of meaning interacting with a process of developing competence.[34] When newcomers arrive, their interest and engagement need to be enabled in order that they might develop and gain recognized competence within the community. "Being included in what matters is a requirement for being engaged in a community's practice, just as engagement is what defines belonging."[35] To be involved in the mutual engagement of a joint enterprise, a newcomer must be granted legitimacy. This legitimacy is, first, the recognition that newcomers are exactly who they are supposed to be, valued for their unique status within the community. It is an acknowledgment that their presence is legitimate. Second, to validate and support this legitimacy, a newcomer must have access to resources and people and to the joint enterprise that binds those resources and people within the community of practice. Lave and Wenger's study of apprenticeship revealed this point most clearly:

> Apprentice quartermasters not only have access to the physical activities going on around them and to the tools of the trade; they participate in information flows and conversations, in a context in which they can make sense of what they observe and hear. In focusing on the epistemological role of artifacts in the context of social organization of knowledge, [the] notion of transparency constitutes, as it were, the cultural organization of access. . . . Thus, the term transparency when used here in connection with technology refers to the way in which using artifacts and understanding their significance interact to become one learning process.[36]

Newcomers need access in order to participate in a community of practice. In the catechumenate, sponsors provide access for newcomers. Sponsors not only "show a way" but also provide a buffer for newcomers to ask questions and make mistakes. "Granting newcomers legitimacy is important because they are likely to come short of what the community regards as competent engagement. Only with enough legitimacy can all their inevitable stumblings and violations become opportunities for learning rather than cause for dismissal, neglect, or exclusion."[37] Sponsors are asked to share in all newcomer-welcoming activities with the newcomers. They are also asked to worship with them and stand alongside them during each public rite that occurs during the worship service. If the sponsors participate in service activities with the congregation, they should consider inviting the newcomers to participate in that service with them. Keeping in touch with the newcomers weekly, they should check in by phone or e-mail regularly and try to meet face-to-face outside of group activities on occasion, perhaps at a work setting. The role of sponsor is to listen, befriend, guide, and support the questions and discernment of the newcomer, recognizing that the sponsor will not have all the answers but can share experiences in their own life as a Christian.

As important as the role of sponsors is for the newcomer in the catechumenate process, it is remarkable that nearly every sponsor I interviewed downplayed his role and responsibility in light of how much he gained from the process and how much he learned from the newcomer. The experience of sponsoring is one of mutual participation and identity formation for both sponsor and newcomer in the catechumenate process.

LEGITIMATE PERIPHERAL PARTICIPATION

In terms of the theory of legitimate peripheral participation, I have explored the importance of legitimacy in relationship to the access newcomers need to enable participation. I have also looked at the dynamics of participation and reification, which form the newcomer's identity within a community of practice through mutual engagement around a joint enterprise with access to shared resources. Now I will turn to the importance of peripheral participation.

Peripherality enables newcomers to observe actively. It involves participation, but even more, it values an extended period of time to explore what is the discipleship task, who is involved, and which resources are available for use. Peripherality offers the newcomer agency with regard to participation and learning. Newcomers in participatory situations explore the practice on their own terms with regard for their own life experience and relationship to the community of practice. Lave and Wenger explain, "For newcomers then the purpose is not to learn *from* talk as a substitute for legitimate peripheral participation: it is to learn *to* talk as a key to legitimate peripheral participation."[38] When newcomers have the promise of full access and increasing participation within the community of practice, there is motivation for learning.

Because of the inherent instability of practice as an emergent structure located in the negotiation of mutual engagement, there is a need to attend to and design what it takes to ensure cohesion. Practice emerges over time through participation. Although attention can be given to learning design, practice itself or the learning involved in practice cannot be designed directly: "One can articulate patterns or define procedures . . . one can design systems of accountability and policies . . . one can design roles . . . one can design visions . . . one can design work processes . . . one can design curriculum. One can attempt to institutionalize a community of practice, but the community of practice itself will slip through the cracks and remain distinct from its institutionalization . . . . Learning cannot be designed: it can only be designed for—that is, facilitated or frustrated."[39] Since communities of practice are emergent, involving mutual engagement, a joint enterprise, and shared resources, participation is integral for learning. Learning about participation is not as effective as learning through participation. Designing learning involves the constant attention to patterns, procedures, systems of accountability and policies, roles, visions, processes, and curriculum. These are the aspects of learning to which we can give attention.

A Cruciform Catechesis

I can now restate what I said earlier. Designing a theory of social learning for communities of practice to support newcomer identity, participation, and belonging is an essential task for congregations. One of the key strengths of the catechumenate's design for newcomer welcome is the opportunity it allows for newcomers to take time for meaningful and formational catechesis. What happened in Annie's experience with the Seekers comes into clear focus. Congregations are designing newcomer-welcoming processes that encouraging newcomers to establish their identity in relationship with oldcomers (sponsors, catechists, and congregational leaders), which in turn fosters a sense of belonging to the congregation.

The learning that leads to a change in behavior is not happening by chance. Exploring the theory of legitimate peripheral participation, pastors and catechists now have language to facilitate the complicated dynamic between newcomers and oldcomers. Communities of practice involve the mutual engagement of participants, both newcomers and oldcomers, in discipleship tasks over time that create resources for negotiating meaning and constructing individual and corporate identity within the *ecclesia crucis*.[40] Over time and in relationship to each other and the reified resources of the community of practice, newcomers and oldcomers gradually develop competence through their recognition that they need each other. No one possesses the action or the meaning that arises from the interaction within the gathering. A catechesis that is shared mutually among all participants, in which everyone's knowledge is partial and incomplete, and that values the competence of the other as equal to and sometimes even more important than the competence of those who are already present is a cruciform catechesis.

This cruciform catechesis gives rise to the *ecclesia crucis*, and the *ecclesia crucis* shapes a cruciform catechesis. Newcomers and oldcomers recognize their discipleship on the way as shaped by their mutual commitment to the task of figuring it out. At the same time, the *ecclesia crucis* becomes the locus—the space—in which communities of practice arise by designing opportunities for learning through a cruciform catechesis. In theory, this ministry of welcoming newcomers attempts to balance the movement of a disestablished community within congregations while offering a clear and intentionally designed process to facilitate newcomer welcome, learning, and participation. In the next chapter, I explore the challenges that still discourage newcomer welcome in congregations and identify the ways congregational leaders can respond.

Notes

1. Jean Lave and Etienne Wenger, *Situated Learning: Legitimate Peripheral Participation,* Learning in Doing: Social, Cognitive, and Computational Perspectives, ed. John Seely Brown (Cambridge: Cambridge University Press, 1991), 15.

2. "Learning is a source of social structure." In making this claim, Wenger is navigating the duality of structure and agency that remains *the* question at the heart of social theory. Wenger aligns himself most closely with Anthony Giddens's theory of structuration. Giddens's structuration theory is based on the idea "that structure is both input and output of human actions, that actions have both intended and unintended consequences, and that actors know a great deal but not everything about the structural ramifications of their actions." Ibid., 96, 281. Giddens, like Wenger, begins by exploring the knowledgeability of agents and the constitution of social practice as human being and human doing. However, Giddens's critics accuse him of "underemphasizing the constraining aspects of structure." J. B. Thompson and Margaret Archer are two of Giddens's strongest critics from this perspective. Lars Bo Kaspersen, *Anthony Giddens: An Introduction to a Social Theorist,* trans. Steven Sampson (Malden, MA: Blackwell, 2000), 160–62. Wenger attempts to address Giddens's critics in his own theory by way of Pierre Bourdieu's work: "[Bourdieu] uses the concept of practice to counter purely structuralist or functionalist accounts of culture and to emphasize the generative character of structure by which cultural practices embody class relations . . . . [Bourdieu] argues that practices are generated from an underlying structure, which he calls the *habitus.* In my [Wenger's] argument the *habitus* would be an emerging property of interacting practices rather than their generative infrastructure, with an existence unto itself. This position is closer to Giddens's notion of structuration, but with practices as specific contexts for the knowledgeability of actors." Etienne Wenger, *Communities of Practice: Learning, Meaning, and Identity,* Learning in Doing: Social Cognitive, and Computational Perspectives, ed. John Seely Brown (Cambridge: Cambridge University Press, 1998), 281–82, 289.

3. Lave and Wenger, *Situated Learning,* 31.

4. Ibid., 33.

5. Wenger, *Communities of Practice,* 138.

6. Ibid., 3. Lave and Wenger are insistent that their theory of situated learning called legitimate peripheral participation is not an educational form, pedagogical strategy, or teaching technique. Lave and Wenger, *Situated Learning,* 40.

7. Wenger, *Communities of Practice,* 72–85.

8. Ibid., 56.

9. Ibid., 165.

10. Ibid., 56.

11. Ibid., 277. Italics mine.

12. Ibid.

13. Ibid., 64.

14. Ibid., 102.

15. Wenger defines meaning as "a way of talking about our (changing) ability—individually and collectively—to experience our life and world as meaningful." Ibid., 5. William F. Hanks writes in the forward of Wenger's book with Jean Lave, "Once we see discourse production as a

social and cultural practice, and not as a second-order representation of practice, it becomes clear that it must be configured along with other kinds of work in the overall matrix of performance." Lave and Wenger, *Situated Learning*, 22–23.

16. Wenger, *Communities of Practice*, 52–53.

17. Ibid., 54.

18. Etienne Wenger, Richard McDermott, and William M. Snyder, *Cultivating Communities of Practice: A Guide to Managing Knowledge* (Boston: Harvard Business School Press, 2002), 36.

19. Wenger, *Communities of Practice*, 5.

20. Nancy Ammerman has argued that the de facto way individuals practice religion in North America is to gather within communities of faith through congregational organization: "American religion has thrived not because it has freed each individual to pursue his or her own spiritual quest or because uniquely viable theological ideas have taken root here, but because American law and society have created a space for voluntary religious communities. Those local congregations stand at the heart of the pragmatic religious life that flourishes here. People gather to sustain spiritual life and accomplish valuable work. What they experience in congregations may shape their families, vocations, politics, and leisure in new ways." Nancy Tatom Ammerman, *Pillars of Faith: American Congregations and Their Partners* (Berkeley: University of California Press, 2005), 2.

21. Noting that people knew where to find houses of worship on September 11, 2001, Christian educator Norma Cook Everist writes, "The faith community's curriculum is much more than material on paper to be read and recited; it embraces all of the people in this time and context as well as people in God's global and historic community." Norma Cook Everist, *The Church as Learning Community: A Comprehensive Guide to Christian Education* (Nashville: Abingdon, 2002), 9.

22. Wenger, *Communities of Practice*, 95.

23. Ibid., 77.

24. Ibid., 78.

25. Ibid.

26. Ibid.

27. Ibid., 152.

28. Ibid.

29. Ibid., 83.

30. Ibid., 275.

31. Ibid., 276.

32. Ibid.

33. Ibid., 157–58.

34. Wenger, *Communities of Practice*, 138.

35. Ibid., 74.

36. Lave and Wenger, *Situated Learning*, 102.

37. Wenger, *Communities of Practice*, 101.

38. Lave and Wenger, *Situated Learning*, 109.

39. Wenger, *Communities of Practice*, 229.

40. Ibid., 72–85.

4

Designing Disestablishment

Beth moved to a small university town in Pennsylvania because her boyfriend was attending law school. Since her boyfriend had grown up Lutheran, they began visiting the local Lutheran church. She said, "People always came up to us and talked to us. We felt very welcomed. I've had this sense that this is home for us now." I asked Beth to share why she and her boyfriend started visiting this Lutheran church.

I always missed out on church because my family didn't go. My grandparents—one side goes, and one side doesn't. I never had a religious background. I just decided that that was something I wanted to do. And I wanted to be baptized before I was married. The more I asked questions to different people and figure out which religion I wanted to go with, I felt that this was the most welcoming place.

My boyfriend's father was baptized on the day he was married. He talked to me about adult baptism. I knew that there was going to be some time and effort put into this. Why keep talking about it and just do it? So I made a New Year's resolution to be baptized. Right after January, we came in and talked to Pastor and asked him, "What do we need to do?" He said, "We have a way." Within a week, my catechist called, and we've been meeting ever since.

Our meetings are very informal—in [my catechist's] home and in a setting like this [motioning to the small meeting room in the church] when my sponsor comes with me. One night I asked why there were different versions of the Bible. I didn't get any of this. I felt like a five-year-old going into this. I have no religious background. She explained part of it and talked about translating it into more recent vocabulary. One night she used three or four different Bibles to show me the different translations.

Then I saw the difference. That was neat, because you could hear some of the language and realize that is really not how we talk today, so I could understand the difference.

I asked Beth what her baptism was like. She responded:

It was really neat. The actual process was relaxing, comforting; it was nice to finally get to that point. But I was really surprised. I knew it was a big deal, but I didn't realize the entire magnitude of it until it happened. I told my friend that I was getting baptized, and I got a card from him. It was so special that so many people recognized my baptism. I just wanted everyone to come to my house for a dinner and come to the Easter Vigil. Then everyone brought gifts, ornaments, and books. I didn't realize the magnitude of it until that night. It was so cool, because after we came back from church, it was after nine. I thought people would just go home, but everyone stayed until twelve or one. I thought everyone would leave, but I was glad they stayed!

Beth explained to me that one book she received was particularly meaningful:

One lady I work with gave me The Purpose Driven Life. *We were talking about it, and I told her I was going to be baptized. She left the book and a note on my desk, saying congratulations. She's older. Sixty-two, I think. For years and years, she had been going to church twenty minutes away from her house, and more recently she left to go to a local church. She decided to now become a member of that church from the impetus of my baptism. That was really meaningful to me.*

Beth's story is highly unusual within Lutheran churches. She was a newcomer who was not only unchurched but unbaptized as well. When she arrived at this small Lutheran church in central Pennsylvania, she and her boyfriend felt welcomed. She had been considering baptism for some time. Through the catechumenate process, this elusive practice called baptism became meaningful, not only through the rite and through the encounters with her sponsor and catechist, but also through a woman at her workplace, who made an important decision of her own because Beth testified to her experience within the catechumenate process.

As our interview closed, Beth wondered how long she would be able to stay within this community. Her boyfriend lived in the neighborhood, but she worked nearly an hour away. As I listened to her reflect on the meaning of baptism and its importance in her life, particularly in relation to her coworker, I saw a quiet determination to stay as long as she could within this congregation. She was no longer a liminal because the newcomer-welcome process had shaped her Christian identity as a disciple in a consistent way; her faith shaped her practices and her practices strengthened her faith.

As one of only a few newcomers to step over the threshold of this congregation, Beth became visibly recognized by many in the congregation through the public rites. But she was not known and did not have many interactions with oldcomers beyond those with her sponsor and catechist. At the time of our interview she had still not untied the ribbon on her hand-calligraphed scroll of the Apostles' Creed, given to her in one of those public rites. I wondered if that tied-up scroll was a metaphor for her own Christian identity and her relationship with the congregation. Establishment congregations tend to give newcomers the impression that the conclusion of the newcomer-welcoming process inevitably means a newcomer has established his or her identity as a Christian and has established his or her membership within the congregation. To other oldcomers, Beth was now one of them. And yet, she wasn't. Beth didn't necessarily "know" these oldcomers. Beth's baptism and the process of becoming a disciple had led her to experience the fluidity of Christian identity and the importance of continuing to figure it out throughout her life. With whom now was she to continue this joint enterprise, this task within the congregation?

Like Maly's church, Beth's congregation is one I would characterize as established. Beth's disestablished posture was not mirrored in the established membership of the congregation outside of her sponsor and catechist. In the congregations I researched, leaders and pastors are tending to a cruciform catechesis and the interactions between newcomers and oldcomers *within* the newcomer-welcoming process but not facilitating relationships beyond those boundaried and distinct catechumenal communities. To design a wider congregational disestablishment, leaders, including the pastor, are responsible for facilitating relationships between newcomers and oldcomers within all the congregation's communities of practice.

Problems with Newcomer Assimilation

I have refrained from the use of the word *assimilation*, preferring instead to use the language of facilitating newcomer participation and belonging. However, most of the literature on newcomers describes assimilation as a linear process moving the newcomer from the periphery to the core.[1] The main thesis of Lyle Schaller's book *Assimilating New Members*, written in 1978, is that congregations need "a broader-based, more active and more intentional system" for reaching, receiving, accepting, and assimilating new members. [2] To facilitate this process, congregations need to support newcomer entry through small groups, or as he calls them, face-to-face groups.

Schaller identifies four routes by which newcomers are encouraged to participate in a congregation. First, he notes that newcomers might already be a part of a subgroup within the congregation, thus establishing a meaningful relationship before formally joining the congregation. Routes into the congregation via subgroups open up when newcomers have a friend (or an oldcomer) who can facilitate their participation in the community of practice or because the newcomer brings an expertise or interest in the subgroup and can join with competence. The challenge of the latter way of joining a subgroup arises when the newcomer does not have an oldcomer willing to help her navigate the reified resources of the current community. Unfortunately, most subgroups function in established ways that do not anticipate the participation of newcomers, so a newcomer without an oldcomer's support will find his disarticulations unwelcomed and unsettling for the community of practice.

A second way to enter a congregation, Schaller would argue, is by joining a group within the congregation immediately after the formal membership process. The challenges I saw most often in the catechumenate process were with this route. In fact, in one instance, a newcomer group decided to ease their own transition into existing groups within the congregation by circumventing the process entirely. After they formally joined the congregation, they formed their own young-adult group. They immediately went in search of other young-adult members of the congregation and invited these oldcomers to join them. But the result of adding oldcomers, who held different ideas as to how the group should function, to the close-knit group of new members, who already held a reified notion of what they wanted out of the group, the combined group developed factions and ultimately broke apart in anger and frustration. The pastor and the catechist at this congregation wish they had stepped in earlier to address the conflict.

Attending to the transition from newcomer to lifelong learner of the Christian faith is similar to attending to the confirmand's transition from child to adult in the congregation. Yet in these cases too, mainline Protestant congregations are generally unable to adequately transition newly baptized or confirmed members from highly intense and deeply personal periods of catechesis into the daily life of congregational membership. Henry and Beth were both anxious as to how they would "join" another group after their newcomer-welcoming process was complete. Henry had a way. Beth's way was not as clear. The difference was again due to the congregation's relationship with establishment and disestablishment.

Schaller's third route is for the newcomer to assume, rather quickly, a role or office within the congregation: "This might be as a Sunday school teacher, counselor for a youth group, leader of a circle in the woman's organization, treasurer of a Sunday school class, usher, president of the men's group, trustee, or member of the governing body of that parish."[3] Newcomers who have experience as full and active participants in a prior congregation most often take this route. The challenge with this route is similar to the newcomer arriving with expertise in the first route. Without an oldcomer or congregational leader's guidance, the newcomer will not learn the reified resources and may find his disarticulations thwarted by oldcomers. New staff and new pastors also find themselves in this position when joining a congregation for the first time.

A final route for a newcomer to establish a relationship with congregation is for the newcomer "to accept a task or job as a worker."[4] This route is the most compelling for me, because Schaller recognizes that what is central to a community is its task. A social learning theory would support the movement into a congregation through a task but demand attention to the relationship between newcomers and oldcomers within the task.

Schaller does reflect on another possible route. He says, "The remainder of the new adult members do not fit into any of these four categories. Most of them either have or are in the process of dropping into comparative inactivity."[5] In other words, these newcomers have been marginalized.

Welcome, orient, and then assimilate by offering the newcomer a spiritual-gifts inventory, followed by an invitation to serve on committees or in a specific role, is a norm so often repeated in newcomer and evangelism books. This linear process sounds easy, but it is actually not helpful. Orientation or training sessions, although necessary, cannot effectively prepare newcomers for participation in communities of practice, because in these classes, newcomers are separate from oldcomers and the discipleship practices of this local congregation.

Schaller makes an important argument that inviting newcomers to join an existing small group or assume a task or role is exactly what needs to happen in congregations *as long as* oldcomers are attentive to their role of facilitating newcomer participation. Unfortunately, more often, congregational leaders pour so much energy into the orientation session and following up with matching newcomers with a group, task, or role that little time is given to the dynamic and complex negotiation that happens after newcomers join a community of practice or assume a new task or role. And even with a deliberate newcomer-welcoming process in place, newcomers still described the transition from the protective and structured environment of the catechumenate to life in the congregation post-catechumenate as scary.

PARTICIPATION TRAJECTORIES

Newcomers are not "joining" a static group of people and thus do not need to be "assimilated" or "socialized." Rather, newcomers are on the way toward becoming peripheral or full participants in communities who contribute to the evolution of the practice as they learn alongside oldcomers, who also are "on the way." Further, as demonstrated in the last chapter, congregations are made up of multiple communities of practice. Every time an oldcomer moves from one community to another, the oldcomer becomes a newcomer. Identifying one's trajectory of participation offers a more comprehensive strategy for supporting communities of practice in congregations and the mutual engagement that surrounds the joint enterprises of those communities. Wenger identifies five trajectories of participation that are intimately bound to the ongoing work of identity formation in a community of practice:

> *Peripheral trajectories.* By choice or by necessity some trajectories never lead to full participation. Yet they may well provide a kind of access to a community and its practice that becomes significant enough to contribute to one's identity.
>
> Inbound *trajectories.* Newcomers are joining the community with the prospect of becoming full participants in its practice. Their identities are invested in their future participation, even though their present participation may be peripheral.
>
> Insider *trajectories.* The formation of an identity does not end with full membership. The evolution of the practice continues—new events, new demands, new inventions, and new generations all create occasions for renegotiating one's identity.
>
> Boundary *trajectories.* Some trajectories find their value in spanning boundaries and linking communities of practice. Sustaining an

identity across boundaries is one of the most delicate challenges of this kind of brokering work.

Outbound trajectories. Some trajectories lead out of a community, as when children grow up. What matters then is how a form of participation enables what comes next. It seems perhaps more natural to think of identity formation in terms of all the learning involved in entering a community of practice. Yet being on the way out of such a community also involves developing new relationships, finding a different position with respect to the community, and seeing the world and oneself in new ways.[6]

Wenger's five trajectories have significant applicability to newcomers, oldcomers, congregational leaders, and pastors in a congregational setting. This framework recognizes the dynamic and ever-evolving nature of communities for all who are involved. First and foremost, insiders are never static, in Wenger's proposal. Insiders, or what I have been referring to as oldcomers, are also on a trajectory tending the joint enterprise of the community by responding to "new events, new demands, new inventions, and new generations" and renegotiating their participation in different ways. There is a case to be made that all participants in the *ecclesia crucis* should have outbound trajectories, being called to meaningful engagement on the periphery with newcomers and the world. Later in this chapter I will explore the boundary trajectories of congregational and pastoral leaders working to link various communities of practice within and beyond the congregation.

The catechumenate process involves newcomers and their sponsors, catechists, congregational leaders, and pastors. Four-fifths of the participants in this process are oldcomers who might seem to be insiders. In truth, some sponsors and catechists are insiders, but others are not, and some congregational leaders always remain on the boundary, even as others remain inside. Describing the dynamism, the movement, of the *ecclesia crucis* is one way to make Beth's commitment to the ongoing task of figuring out what discipleship means, a legitimate trajectory in a congregation. To expose newcomers and oldcomers alike to a variety of possible trajectories is to enable their imagination of what participation might look like.[7] I imagine there were a few oldcomers in Beth's congregation who could identify with a peripheral, inbound, or outbound trajectory and invite her to participate peripherally in new tasks within and beyond the congregation. And more, Beth's involvement in new tasks would put her back again on an inbound trajectory learning how to participate in a new community of practice.

Peripheral participation is a legitimate meaningful way to participate in a community of practice. By lingering—legitimately—on the periphery, newcomers (and, indeed, some sponsors as well) can observe and make meaning out of both the biographies of current oldcomers and the reified stories of members who are gone. "A community of practice is a history collapsed into a present that invites engagement. Newcomers can engage with their own potential future as embodied by old-timers. As a community of practice, these old-timers deliver the past and offer the future, in the form of narratives and participation both. Each has a story to tell."[8] Using the narrative trajectories of oldcomers, newcomers will forge their own trajectories by adopting, modifying, or rejecting the old possibilities.

Sponsors and catechists who shared their stories with me said over and over how much they needed this process. Their own sense of belonging to the congregation and participating in the worship and small groups for study and reflection was transformed through the process. I noticed that some of these sponsors and catechists who might be considered oldcomers to those in the congregation did not consider themselves insiders. Wenger notes that identity within and across a community of practice is a constant becoming: "The work of identity is always going on. Identity is not some primordial core of personality that already exists. Nor is it something we acquire at some point in the same way that, at a certain age, we grow a set of permanent teeth. Even though issues of identity as a focus of overt concern may become more salient at certain times than at others, our identity is something we constantly renegotiate during the course of our lives."[9] Shelly's story is a case in point.

In my research, Shelly, a sponsor for a young woman who had not yet been baptized, recalled being "shocked" when the pastor asked her to be a sponsor: "I was like, 'Why me?' I did not think I was the ideal candidate at that time in my life to be sponsoring someone. But other people know better than you do. Pastor knew that it was something I needed as well." Shelly had grown up in this congregation but major complications in her family's life led her to participate infrequently. During the catechumenate process Shelly increased her participation, attending both the catechumenate sessions and worship weekly. I asked Shelly to describe one of the most important moments of the catechumenal process and she chose her catechumen's baptism. Specifically she spoke about the water at baptism.

The water. The water being shared. We allow water to move here when we are baptizing. Those around also get wet. This is the first place that I had ever experienced that. Even with our infant baptisms, the water is very free flowing. There is usually water on the floor. The sharing of the water and the word and the overflowing of it means a lot to me. Other people may not get that. I still get chills when I see baptisms today. And I always sit up front. I'm experiencing it again, every time there is one. That sounds corny to some people. I had a lot—I had a very rocky road to get to where my faith is today. Being involved in the catechumenate brought things back into focus for me. Worship is . . . I'm not real active in the church, . . . but worship is the number one thing for me. . . . I have to be here. When there is a baptism, it's a renewing [of my faith] all over again for me.[10]

Once the catechumenal process ended, Shelley's insider trajectory morphed again as she moved back into peripheral participation. Shelly's life circumstances could not lead her to hold an insider trajectory. However, her temporary participation as an insider greatly enhanced her Christian identity and her ongoing peripheral participation. She identified her participation in the catechumenate process as bringing things back into focus and renewing her commitment to worship. Shelly maintains the possibility that if and when the circumstances of her life change, she may participate more fully in the life of the congregation. The newcomer-welcoming process certainly shaped her sense of identity as a Christian and belonging to her congregation. For now, however, she is content to remain on the periphery.

PARTICIPATION TRAJECTORIES IN COMMUNITIES OF PRACTICE

Although Shelly continued to come to worship fairly regularly, once the process of welcoming newcomers ended, she did not join another group within the congregation. How do we recognize Shelly's ongoing peripheral participation as legitimate? This is a question congregations often face as members move from one trajectory of participation to another depending upon their life circumstances. Yet Shelly's participation also lends itself to another aspect of communities of practice. Individuals do not belong to or participate in only one community of practice. In fact, Shelly's broader network of family and work had her involved in many distinct communities of practice outside the congregation. Often, congregations would consider Shelly to be an inactive member (or what some might call a "Christmas and Easter Christian"). Given that her sense of belonging is strong and her identity as a Christian has been shaped and formed in a congregation, do we recognize her larger family sphere as a part of a Christian way of life—existing, perhaps, at the boundary? Is this not the location of Christian discipleship practice situated at the point of dissolution and disarticulation, waiting opportunity for reinterpretation? Is this not the boundary between Christian and non-Christian practices where Christian identity is discerned—not disengaged, but engaged? Shelly's boundary was between the church and her family. Her role as a sponsor encouraged Shelly to reinterpret her identity as a Christian in light of her role in her family and outside the church.

Henry's boundary, in contrast, was the threshold of the church. Henry's involvement within the congregation continued after the catechumenate through his making and serving dinners in the church kitchen. He began to participate within the community of practice that made meals for the children's programming on Wednesday evenings. Having already experienced the meals during the catechumenate program on Sunday evenings, Henry felt competent moving into this community of practice, and the members of the kitchen committee whom he had already met on Sunday evenings facilitated his participation. His role as newcomer encouraged Henry to reinterpret his identity as a Christian in light of service within the church.

Disestablished congregations encourage legitimate peripheral participation and full participation equally in order to facilitate a sense of belonging among their members. Sometimes participation trajectories will lead newcomers and oldcomers toward full participation in the church, and sometimes participation trajectories will lead newcomers and oldcomers toward legitimate peripheral participation at the boundary of the church and the world. To be a Christian church is to practice being a people under the cross. The *ecclesia crucis* forms members for life in *and* beyond the local congregation. The movement does not come from individuals or even the courage of people, but rather from the movement of God toward the world in Jesus Christ. The *ecclesia crucis* exists not to live but to die in being sent and scattered, propelled out into the world. This is foolishness.

FACILITATING MULTIMEMBERSHIP

Congregations are not only *one* community of practice, and neither are the ascetic monasteries. Congregations are made up of multiple communities of practice or subcommunities, so oldcomers and newcomers alike must constantly negotiate multimemberships. Oldcomers and newcomers, like Shelly, also interact with multiple communities outside of the church. Multimembership inside and outside the church is complex. It connotes multiple trajectories, modes of engagement, experiences of participation and nonparticipation, competencies, and ultimately the potential for multiple identities. The work of reconciling multiple identities across various communities of practice may never be completely resolved.[11]

Congregations need to recognize this reality of multimembership across subcommunities as integral to the process of identity formation. Identity itself is diverse in various settings and requires attention and work to reconcile. Wenger writes, "In other words, by including processes of reconciliation in the very definition of identity, I am suggesting that the maintenance of an identity across boundaries requires work and, moreover, that the work of integrating our various forms of participation is not just a secondary process. This work is not simply an additional concern for an independently defined identity viewed as a unitary object; rather, it is at the core of what it means to be a person. Multimembership and the work of reconciliation are intrinsic to the very concept of identity."[12]

The tension felt in reconciling multimemberships is present in all the stages of the newcomer-welcoming process. Catechists/pastors, as established members, feel the tension in helping newcomers cross a bridge between being in the newcomer group and being (established) members. Sponsors feel this tension because their encounters with newcomers change their own experiences of meaning and competence in relationship to the larger congregation. And as already noted, newcomers themselves feel a heightened anxiety as multimembership is encouraged toward the end of the newcomer-welcoming process.

Newcomers who have moved to full participation in the newcomer community of practice become newcomers again as they seek to participate in other ongoing communities of practice within the congregation. The newcomers' experience of anxiety at the end of the welcoming process is heightened if their full participation and competence are recognized only within the newcomer community of practice and nowhere else within the congregation. If the newcomers' community of practice dissipates (which it is created to do), where will the newcomers' identity, belonging, participation, and competence be located? This issue needs attention long before the newcomer-welcoming process ends. It can be addressed by encouraging multimembership.

Recognizing and attending the boundaries of these communities within the congregation is the responsibility of the pastor and congregational leaders. Newcomers such as Henry need to be assured that pastors, catechists, and sponsors will guide their transition before, during, and after the newcomer-welcoming process. This attending involves making connections and building bridges between communities of practice to enable individuals to navigate their multiple trajectories and identities. Wenger has identified two types of connections, one of which is reified and the other participatory. The reified connections are called boundary objects. The participatory connections are identified as brokering.

BOUNDARY OBJECTS

Boundary objects, according to Wenger, are "artifacts, documents, terms, concepts, and other forms of reification around which communities of practice can organize their interconnections."[13] Church constitutions might be considered boundary objects, for these documents serve to connect various communities of practice within a congregation. Other boundary objects might be the pictorial directory, the welcome brochure, the mission statement, the history of the move from one building to another, and the story behind the ugly carpet in the parlor. Many congregations have created a spiritual-gifts inventory, which potentially serves as a boundary object to clarify which communities of practice might interest a newcomer. Some congregations might go a step further by producing ministry descriptions for these communities of practice to facilitate the participation of newcomers in various ministries, committees, events, and so on.

Wenger notes the importance of boundary objects for their ability to transcend the limits of participation. For instance, a worship bulletin or a recording of the service can be sent to a homebound member of a congregation in order to facilitate the member's sense of belonging to a community in which she cannot longer participate regularly. Wenger writes, "We cannot be all over the world, but we can read the newspaper. We cannot live in the past, but we can wonder at monuments left behind by long-gone practices."[14]

Reified boundary objects are certainly abstracted, modular, accommodating and standardized,[15] yet because of these characteristics, they enable connections and transcend multiple communities of practice. For instance, the narthex (entryway) of a congregation might serve as the nexus of multiple communities of practice in any given week. The youth committee might be asking for donations to fund a mission trip, while the ushers are passing out bulletins on Sunday morning. The Sunday school might display the children's most recent art creations, while the stewardship committee hopes to unveil its newest campaign. The evangelism committee might propose a space to help facilitate the worship experience for parents who need to leave worship momentarily with their children, which leads the property committee to spend time in the space, wondering about what to do. Each of these groups is a community of practice within the congregation. Each of these groups needs access to the narthex. Thus, the narthex becomes a hub of activity where connections and accommodations are made both implicitly and explicitly between the various communities and where boundaries need to be managed with attention.

Managing the use of the narthex as shared space among many constituencies might take the form of a written document created by the property committee in connection with the church leadership and pastor. It may be one piece of paper among many placed within a leadership manual that all the congregational leaders received at an orientation session when they became leaders. Such a document would be a boundary object. However, as noted before, reliance on paper or trainings is never enough.

BROKERING

Because the boundary objects are insufficient on their own, Wenger identifies the need for participatory or people connections to travel with those objects. Wenger calls these people connections "brokers," borrowing the term from his colleague Penelope Eckert.[16] Brokers facilitate connections between communities of practice, introducing elements of one practice into another.[17] In disestablished congregations, congregational leaders, staff, and pastors in particular function as brokers by attending to the connections and the learning that occurs at the boundaries of distinct communities of practice. Some people seem to thrive on being brokers: "they love to create connections and engage in 'import-export,' and so would rather stay at the boundaries of many practices than move to the core of any one practice."[18]

The job of the broker is very complex, because it involves enough participation in a practice and awareness of that practice without becoming fully absorbed in only that one practice. Pastors felt this tug within their newcomer-welcoming processes as they shifted greater attention to the welcome process during its initial design and implementation. Oldcomers who had had the pastor's full participation in their communities of practice before the implementation of the newcomer-welcoming process experienced the pastor's growing absences with frustration and concern. Pastors who handled this transition by being conscious of the feelings of oldcomers while also consciously facilitating transactions between the newcomers and established communities of practice tended to have broader support for the newcomer initiatives.

Another complexity of the broker is the importance of having legitimacy among various communities.[19] Cultivating this legitimacy requires enough participation to know the language and shared resources, the basics of the joint enterprise, and the general meanings that arise from the community's sustained mutual engagement. Wenger notes that this legitimacy enables the broker "to influence the development of a practice, mobilize attention, and address conflicting interests."[20] With this legitimacy in hand, brokers are able to link practices by introducing elements of one practice into another's practice.[21] Much as newcomers influence a community of practice, brokers exert influence by spurring the evolution of the practice as new resources are introduced, new tasks are assumed, and broader meanings about such tasks are encountered. For instance, the broker may introduce a new stewardship idea used successfully in another congregation, which might take the stewardship committee's joint enterprise in an entirely new direction and lead the members to new ideas of what it means to enable and facilitate stewardship in the congregation.

Brokers are also essential to establishing boundary practices. When a pastor establishes an ongoing Bible study for leaders of the congregation who serve on all sorts of various ministries, a boundary practice has been created. A community of practice with all of its constituent elements exists but with the intention of gathering disparate members of various communities to an ongoing task. Brokers may not establish ongoing relationships between communities of practice but may facilitate the coordination for a one-time event or enable opportunities for meetings between one or two individuals.

Brokers may also open a community of practice at the periphery to enable the participation of newcomers. This is a crucial responsibility of sponsors, catechists, and pastors in disestablished congregations to encourage ongoing communities of practice other than the newcomer-welcoming community to enable legitimate peripheral participation within their practice for those newcomers to the community. This needs to happen throughout the newcomer-welcoming process, never only when it ends. Even if a newcomer does not engage in the practice fully until after the newcomer process officially ends, the encouragement and access newcomers receive to participate makes a huge difference in their ability to move from the newcomer experience into the life of the larger congregation.

Finally, it is critically important to note that brokering involves alienation and uprootedness, causing a need for recognition and companionship with other brokers to discuss the joint enterprise of brokering. Pastors and catechists, pastors and congregational leaders need to discuss the importance of brokering and the role of brokering in reconciling disparate and discrete communities of practice. Recognizing this precarious position helps me understand why the relationships between pastors and catechists are so strong in disestablished congregations. Pastors and catechists form identities not from engagement in the communities of practice of congregations, but rather in boundary practices that are no less real but still exist in a somewhat liminal space. This becomes even more critical as pastors and congregational leaders take on the responsibility of facilitating additional modes of belonging.

PASTORAL LEADERSHIP

First and foremost, in every congregation I studied, the catechist and pastor were partners in the ministry of welcoming newcomers. Many, if not all, enjoyed being with each other. The ongoing relationship of mutual learning between pastors and catechists is crucial to the practice of newcomer welcome in congregations, for it is by observing the actions of the pastor and catechists that the sponsors take their cues for how to proceed to be in relationship with newcomers. This modeling cannot be left up to chance. Pastors together with catechists need to say explicitly how they relate to one another in ministry. With more attention to the practice of being a catechist and pastor in relationship or a catechist and sponsor in relationship, sponsors can learn how to be in relationship with newcomers.

Pastors play a vital role in matching sponsors and newcomers, since they tend to have the most frequent interactions with oldcomers and newcomers and have some practice at discerning personalities. The match between sponsor and catechumen is very important. Experience has proven that while all of the sponsor-newcomer dyads are single-gender, other characteristics such as age, occupation, and interests matter less than personality traits. Some pastors trust their "intuition" to make the match. Others have conversations with staff members or the catechists or use categories such as "introvert versus extrovert," or "feeling versus thinking" to make the match. A few pastors described their experience of answered prayer as they witnessed matches blossoming between complete strangers and in odd combinations. Of course, when the match fails, pastors watch carefully so as not to make the same mistake a second time.

Pastors are the leaders of a congregation who can invite newcomers to participate in a newcomer-welcoming process in the first place. Some pastors of catechumenate congregations name expectations clearly. "We have a way" is a clear indication that this process is not a choice that can be dismissed lightly. Even though articulating expectations about a process that is very different from the way the average mainline Protestant congregation welcomes newcomers is a challenge for many congregational leaders, newcomers like Annie will come eager to embrace what is offered and willingly engage the process with conviction.

Inevitably, however, some proceed through this process for the wrong reasons. One catechist struggled through a year with a young couple whose life was so complicated and broken that they often missed meetings, showed up late, or listened with only half an ear to the conversation. The catechist realized quickly that the couple were only interested in having their baby baptized and were going through the motions to make that happen. Reflecting on that year with me, the catechist wondered whether she could have told the couple to come back when they were ready. Yet she knew deeply from her interactions with them that they might never be ready. Instead, she remembers praying daily that they would receive something, if only the slight perception that the church would walk with them throughout their life and the life of their child. Too often, though, she doubted even that. In some cases, newcomers will opt out of a newcomer-welcoming process. If the process is not possible for a newcomer, that person might be encouraged to participate in another community of practice or serve as a sponsor in the future.

Leaders as Brokers

How to support participation takes time to learn because it requires deep attention to the boundaries and peripheries of subcommunities. The general atmosphere that bears the concerns among leadership of most mainline Protestant congregations is the anxiousness that members are not involved in more activities. Pastors and leaders spend nearly every meeting dreaming up possibilities to attract newcomers, encourage ministry volunteers, and increase attendance at congregational events and worship. However, these meetings are generally held with "leaders"—those who are already among "the core" of the congregation. In contrast, disestablished congregations, through their insistence that oldcomers offer space and time to those who are new, reverse that practice and in the process change the general atmosphere of the congregation. Instead of insisting that newcomers become a part of the congregational core, oldcomers share themselves and their time at the periphery. Leading at the periphery is where the practice of disestablishment occurs within the *ecclesia crucis*.

Wenger writes, "There is a wisdom of peripherality—a view of community that can be lost to full participants. It includes paths not taken, connections overlooked, choices taken for granted. But this kind of wisdom often remains invisible even to those who hold its potential, because it can easily become marginalized within established regimes of competence."[22] Leading at the periphery requires the same risks that brokering entails, in that leaders cannot fully immerse themselves in one community of practice because of their role in fostering connections between various communities. Leaders working at the boundaries of multiple communities of practice consciously transfer new knowledge from one community of practice to another while at the same time creating boundary objects and practices to align various joint enterprises. The nexus of boundaried communities of practice is where the potential to learn is greatest.

To facilitate the participation of newcomers not only in newcomer communities of practice, but also in the communities throughout the congregation, is the ongoing task of leaders at the periphery. The peripheral position gives leaders a semidetached perspective, allowing them to observe and direct the congregation's varied and often independently acting ministries while attending to the trajectories of belonging that are constantly active and becoming among established membership. This leadership perspective also attempts to ensure the legitimate peripheral participation of newcomers by anticipating and expecting the presence of newcomers, appreciating their presence, reminding the established membership of the newcomers' unique status within the congregation, and designing opportunities for newcomers to learn—to become disciples—alongside oldcomers.

DESIGNING NEWCOMER WELCOME

The first step in designing a newcomer-welcoming process is to welcome the questions of the very next newcomer who crosses the threshold of your congregation. Consider Jesus' call to the disciples. When he said, "Follow me," at least according to the gospel writer Mark, the disciples did so *immediately*. So do not wait. Do not wait until your brochure is finished. Do not wait until your website is public. Do not wait until your membership database is up-to-date. Stop procrastinating. The very next newcomer who arrives in your congregation is bearing a promise for you.

To welcome this newcomer involves three priorities:

1. Listen to the newcomer's questions.
2. Facilitate the newcomer's participation in discipleship practices alongside oldcomers.
3. Take time for the newcomer to learn the reified resources and repertoire of your very particular congregation.

If these three tasks are your priorities to welcome the very next newcomer, then begin to work backward from these three priorities. What needs to happen in your congregation to welcome the newcomer in this way?

LISTEN TO THE NEWCOMER'S QUESTIONS

To listen to your newcomer's questions, you need to find an oldcomer or multiple oldcomers who have skills to listen well. You will need to discern who can listen to this newcomer, keeping the following principles in mind:

- Newcomer questions may not be what you expect. Some questions may be trivial, some may be very weighty, some may be practical, and some may be deeply theological.
- Newcomer questions may challenge what you know to be the case in your congregation or in Christianity. Do not be defensive. Entertaining challenging questions means holding the tension between "my people" and "not my people." Questions will disarticulate oldcomer ways of knowing.
- Oldcomers also will need spaces to explore the questions that disarticulate what they know and how they know it. This space should include the newcomer being careful not to let oldcomer questions take up the space of entertaining the newcomer's questions.

FACILITATE NEWCOMER PARTICIPATION ALONGSIDE OLDCOMERS

To facilitate newcomer participation in discipleship practices alongside oldcomers, you need to find oldcomers who are willing to facilitate newcomer participation in their community of practice. You might design a specific space dedicated to newcomers practicing African Bible Study and prayer, which is what occurs in catechumenate congregations. Or you might discern another central discipleship practice specific to your congregation that aligns nicely with the priorities of newcomer welcome.

You will need to discern how to facilitate newcomer participation in discipleship practices alongside oldcomers, keeping the following questions and principles in mind:

- What discipleship practices, apart from Sunday-morning worship services, are central to the life of your congregation? Do you have a prayer ministry? Do you have a mission trip? Do you have an adult Bible study? Do you have a caregiving ministry?
- Where does learning how to participate in discipleship practices happen in your congregation? Does your congregation talk *about* discipleship practices, or do you practice discipleship? Are practices newcomer-friendly? Can newcomers learn to participate in practices by showing up to the practice?
- Can you identify oldcomers within these practices who are willing to facilitate newcomer participation in this community of practice? Oldcomers facilitating newcomer participation cannot become defensive in response to newcomer questions. Within the practice, newcomers' questions will need to be entertained.
- How do newcomers experience nonparticipation in this discipleship practice? In other words, how do they know they are newcomers and not oldcomers? Have newcomers traditionally been marginalized by this practice? Is peripheral participation legitimately recognized in this community of practice? You can tell that peripheral participation is legitimate if newcomer questions are entertained and allowed to disarticulate the practice.

TAKE TIME FOR LEARNING YOUR CONGREGATION'S REIFIED RESOURCES AND REPERTOIRE

Finally, you must take time for the newcomer to learn the reified resources and repertoire of your very particular congregation. To do this, you will first need to find oldcomers willing to engage the reified resources and repertoire of your congregation. What resources are often called upon and referred to as guides for discipleship practices? Reified resources and repertoire are often found within files or the stories of oldcomers. Sometimes these oldcomers no longer participate in the discipleship practice but still know how the practice originated or how the practice has adapted over time. Sometimes these oldcomers are still participating in the practice but have forgotten or grown weary of telling the story of how the practice originated or how the practice has adapted over time. These oldcomers may need encouragement to retell the story. Some practices no longer have reified resources or repertoire. Participants in these communities of practice may need encouragement to create new resources or repertoire, recognizing that reification is necessary for participation.

What will occur in the telling or retelling of stories or engaging in the reified resources of the community of practice is that the very particular story of the local congregation will become essential to participating in this practice. The practice is local and personal and does not look like any practice anywhere else in the world. Whatever makes it distinct makes it worth learning about. This is a cruciform catechesis.

You will need to discern how to take time for learning to occur between newcomers and oldcomers, keeping the following questions in mind:

- Who among the oldcomers know the stories of how practices originated and developed in your congregation?
- What resources are often called up and referred to as guides for discipleship practices in your congregation? Is the Bible the central resource? Is the congregation's mission statement a consistent resource? Is the congregational constitution a guiding document? Is a catechism, worship book, or confession of faith a guiding frame for practices? Is a certain oldcomer a font of wisdom from the past? Is a certain oldcomer the archivist who keeps old newsletters and bulletins? Perhaps there are ministry descriptions and brochures that describe what happens in a practice. Are those descriptions and brochures consistent with what actually happens in the present, or were they written for a past conception of the practice? (Please notice that this is the reason why we create brochures and attend to websites. These communication resources are created to serve as catechesis between newcomers and oldcomers and ought to be addressed because of a pressing need coming from a newcomer.)
- How often are dress rehearsals and setups for big events used as opportunities to teach the history of a discipleship practice in the congregation? Who among the oldcomers can tell this story?

If the first step of designing a newcomer-welcoming process is to welcome the questions of the very next newcomer who crosses the threshold of your congregation, then the three priorities described here will naturally follow. At the same time, it is necessary to welcome what will feel unsettling. To listen to newcomer questions, facilitate newcomer participation alongside oldcomers, and take time for newcomers to learn the stories and what matters will take courage. This is God's call for the disestablished congregation. To be a Christian church is for the people under the cross to practice a confession of faith, hope, and love, welcoming newcomers into discipleship practices where faith meets doubt, hope meets despair, and love meets the suffering world. Congregations practice faith as they confess their incompleteness without the newcomer in their midst. In the honest confession of entropy, hope becomes tangible in the newcomers who will come and "be-come" members of the congregation. Love becomes tangible as newcomers appear on the threshold of congregations, weary, broken, and worn, searching for meaning, purpose, identity, and new life. Love is the compulsion to welcome these strangers, eager to hear their questions and announcing God's promises for them and not only for ourselves. This love transforms the congregation's orientation toward God and to the world.

Notes

1. The following are a few examples: Roy M. Oswald and Speed B. Leas, *The Inviting Church: A Study of New Member Assimilation* (Washington, DC: Alban Institute, 1987); Gary McIntosh and Glen Martin, *Finding Them, Keeping Them: Effective Strategies for Evangelism and Assimilation in the Local Church* (Nashville: Broadman & Holman, 1992); Chuck Lawless, *Membership Matters: Insights from Effective Churches on New Member Classes and Assimilation* (Grand Rapids, MI: Zondervan, 2005).

2. Lyle E. Schaller, *Assimilating New Members*, Creative Leadership Series, ed. Lyle E. Schaller (Nashville: Abingdon, 1978), 19. The key theme of Schaller's work is the way newcomers experience the dynamics of inclusion and exclusion in congregations and whether newcomers are encouraged to participate in congregational activities. Schaller has been called "the dean of church consultants" by some, and a study by Dennis Olson and William McKinney in 1993 confirmed that Schaller is considered "an authority on congregational life." He is popular among both conservatives and liberals within Protestant circles, offering research and solutions for practical problems facing congregational leadership. Daniel V. A. Olson, "Learning from Lyle Schaller: Social Aspects of Congregations," *Christian Century*, January 27, 1993.

3. Ibid., 76.

4. Ibid., 77.

5. Ibid., 78.

6. Etienne Wenger, *Communities of Practice: Learning, Meaning, and Identity*, Learning in Doing: Social, Cognitive, and Computational Perspectives, ed. John Seely Brown (Cambridge: Cambridge University Press, 1998), 154–55.

7. One might liken the process of identifying participation trajectories with the process of identifying personality types or spiritual gifts.

8. Ibid., 156.

9. Ibid., 154.

10. Ibid., 160.

11. Ibid., 160.

12. Ibid., 161.

13. Wenger, *Communities of Practice*, 105.

14. Ibid., 110.

15. See Wenger's definition of these boundary objects' characteristics, which he borrows from Leigh Starr. Ibid., 107.

16. Wenger notes that Penelope Eckert created this term through her observations of children interacting at school. Being members of multiple communities of practice, children bring ideas, interests, styles, and revelations from one community to another. Ibid., 109, and see 290ff.

17. Ibid., 105.

18. Ibid., 109.

19. Roy Oswald explores this notion in a helpful resource that highlights the delicate transition period when a pastor is the newcomer to a congregation. Roy M. Oswald, *New Beginnings: A Pastorate Start Up Workbook* (Washington, DC: Alban Institute, 1989).

20. Wenger, *Communities of Practice*, 109.

21. Ibid.

22. Ibid., 216.

5

The Task of the *Ecclesia Crucis*

The *ecclesia crucis* gains its purpose and identity in the task of relating to the world. The movement of the *ecclesia crucis* is not away from the world; it is deliberative and purposeful interaction with the world, a deliberate and engaged disestablishment. The *ecclesia crucis* is a gathered people under the cross, compelled to tend holy spaces where question and promise encounter one another, where faith encounters doubt, hope encounters despair, and love encounters the suffering world.

To hear the questions of newcomers within the *ecclesia crucis* is to move toward the world. Encountering the questions and the question bearers as the means of a cruciform grace that they are leads the church under the cross into death and new life. Newcomers embody God's promise in their questions, even as the questions inevitably give rise to more questions among oldcomers. In the presence of newcomers, oldcomers glimpse the promise of God's presence. Thus, at the intersection of the church and the world, newcomers and established members together negotiate their identity as Christians. This identity is not static, just as the *ecclesia crucis* is not static. This identity is fluid. Together with theologian Katherine Tanner, I propose that discipleship formation in the twenty-first century needs to be a task in and of itself. This task is situated within the *ecclesia crucis* through engagement with the newcomer that is engagement with the world.

Shaped by "the Way"

"The way of the cross" describes the twofold Christian experience of dying and rising. That is, the way of the cross takes seriously the human condition, our feeble attempts at our various ways, together with the inescapable experiences of suffering, pain, loss, angst, horror, grief, and shame. The way of the cross embraces our daily encounter with sin and brokenness within the human experience and its myriad effects and assumes the entropic reality of the local congregation. Yet the way of the cross also leads to the empty tomb, that place where death dies and new life is born. The way of the cross is filled with hope and promise, a persistent expectation that grace trumps sin and that life trumps death. The way of the cross recognizes neither sin nor promise as a one-time event, but rather as the daily life struggles under the weight of sin together with the promise of new life ceaselessly proclaimed and provided by God. The whole of the Christian life is one of daily dying and rising, one of being transformed from "my way," "a way," or "our way" into "the way" of the cross.

This cruciform way—the way of the cross—encounters newcomers and established members equally without regarding identity, participation, or belonging as qualifiers. Newcomers and established members are "on the way," and along the diverse ways of their various trajectories, they encounter communities of practice.

As the earlier chapters described, discipleship practices in disestablished congregations are the means of grace, the places where Jesus promises to show up—through the word of God, the sacraments, and within the Christian community. Practicing this way, shaped by the death and resurrection of Jesus Christ within the gathered *ecclesia crucis*, newcomers come to know and identify their life as shaped by daily dying and rising. Thus, as they live out their baptismal vocation, the *ecclesia crucis* is the movement into which they are drawn and from which they receive courage to engage the world. Practicing this way, newcomers are shaped by the way of the cross. Whichever posture they arrived with or whatever trajectory they choose to take, their way becomes cruciform. Their identity, participation, and belonging in relation to communities of practice within a cruciform church, the *ecclesia crucis*, are constantly shaped by central practices of daily dying and rising. At the same time, their identity, participation, and belonging are already marked with the sign of the cross and gathered within the *ecclesia crucis* to be sent out into the world.

CONFESSION OF LOVE

Communities of practice invite participation that involves mutual recognition between the newcomer and established member. This mutuality is life-giving, and Wenger named its power by likening the dynamic to a theorem of love.[1] Within the limits of social theory Wenger lacks the language to reflect on this theorem. Yet it is love that compels a cruciform identity—one that dies so that others might live. The mutuality experienced in the face-to-face encounter between newcomer and established member is the recognition of God's promise to be present. Love becomes tangible within the congregation as newcomers appear at the threshold of congregations, eager to be known and to be invited to belong. Love is the compulsion to welcome these strangers, listening to their questions, which become shared mutually. Over time, this mutuality informs identity and the development of competence within the community of practice.

A confession of love is realized in the mutual engagement and recognition within the community of practice, as explored throughout this book. Yet present within this confession is the danger of becoming insular and rendering the local nature of identity as static. What still needs to be explored is the juxtaposition of a confession of faith and hope that, held together, form our practice of disestablishment and broaden the sense of identity and belonging as disciples.

CONFESSION OF FAITH

Communities of practice are made up of memories. In that the reifications and shared resources that communities of practice encounter are memories of the past, the memory of faithfulness is within the practicing community. However, this memory of faithfulness also transcends the communities of practice within the local congregation and the local congregation itself. The reified memory also recalls the history and practices of the catholic church and situates the congregation within that story.

Juxtaposed to the confession of love found within a community of practice and its face-to-face engagement is the confession of faith. This juxtaposition is a paradox of the past and present. Memory is embodied in the accounts of participants who are established members and in the reified and shared resources valued within the congregation. As newcomers arrive, boundaried communities of practice become aware of the need to give expression to who they are and what they do. Giving expression to their identity and mutual enterprise is an act of remembering and teaching: catechesis. The powerful witness of the biblical story as heard in worship and in group study or the sharing of how the church building was built not only is a representation of the past, but also is re-presented, made present, in the hearing of those who are gathered. This liturgical setting, this re-presenting, is called *anamnesis*. As new and established participants mutually engage the reified forms and shared resources of the congregation, communities of practice are negotiating reinterpretation, which involves disarticulation and distanciation. Without these reified shared resources, the community would lack boundaries, and learning could not take place.

Yet catechesis is not being transmitted in a didactic manner. Rather, a duality is present in the sense that *traditum* (the content of tradition) is always presented together with and in dynamic interaction with *traditio* (the process of transmission). This dynamic is as true for the present as it was in the past. The Bible, catechisms, confessional documents, liturgical books, and histories were once the negotiated meanings that resulted in resources produced in a particular time. Over time, these resources were reified within a participation framework. Through disarticulation and reinterpretation, these resources become a part of who we are today. They also maintain their usefulness because they reach out to us from the past to challenge and shape who we will become through *traditio*. Identifying the *anamnesis, traditum,* and *traditio* at work in the present and past, newcomers and established members within catechumenate communities of practice are invited to mutual engagement and negotiation of meaning, recalling the past with equal dynamism—making present what is past.

Catechists are very important brokers for the confession of faith within the catechumenate communities of practice, so they need full access to the rich "deposit of faith." To fail to equip catechists with the resources and tools necessary to engage the historical dynamism of negotiated resources is to fail them as leaders of the church. Clergy who do not provide access to the resources of the tradition as dynamic productions of a historic community, but rather reduce their content for memorization in the present (or who minimize the contemporary relevance of traditions, be they ancient traditions of the church or cherished traditions of the local congregation), are cutting off communities of practice from being able to align with the memory of the past. Many catechists themselves are not trained to engage the dynamism of traditional Lutheran catechetical tools, particularly Luther's catechisms, in their role as guides and teachers of the faith. Thus, the potential juxtaposition of the community of practice with its past is unrealized. This is in part because the catechists themselves are reluctant (in some cases) and unable (in other cases) to engage the catechisms meaningfully as valuable teaching tools. However, these catechisms are valuable both in the content they share and in their storied role as a sort of pedagogical, theological thread that has united generations of Lutherans—passed from generation to generation since the time of Luther himself.

In the catechumenate literature and its influence on the catechumenate practitioner, formation has been privileged over the language of education, instruction, and teaching. The idea of education has been reduced to transmitted content in a static classroom environment, with the teacher bearing knowledge and power, and the catechisms epitomize this type of education. This highly reductionistic understanding of education limits the catechists' ability to facilitate learning within the newcomer-welcoming process. A social learning process faithful to the strong characteristics that make the catechumenate useful as a practice for welcoming newcomers could strengthen the use of resources as dynamic and not static. A cruciform catechesis takes seriously the need to balance participation and reification in communities of practice. Engaging reified forms as the negotiated but accessible products of past communities of practice provides newcomers and established members a starting place for mutually engaging their own joint enterprise and shared resources. Through this process, many, if not all, reified forms of the past become shared resources within the community of practice.

Congregations desperately need a cruciform catechesis through engagement with a confession of faith to facilitate the participation and belonging of newcomers in dynamic relationship with established members and the central works of a broadly conceived "deposit of faith." This would include the Bible itself, the church's ancient creeds and liturgical foundation, and the catechisms and disciplines of faith developed by later generations that together form an essential corpus of a Lutheran inheritance within the Christian tradition. By articulating a confession of faith, disciples are gathered to recall the story and make present again the joint enterprises and meanings of the past.

Communities of practice are bounded, discrete, and local. To some degree, such communities run the risk of articulating a narrow (bound, discrete, and local) history and experience of meaning. These localized pasts need to be juxtaposed—that is, need to be provided with the opportunity to die and rise to new life—with the broader memory of faith within the congregation. Whether it is through membership in multiple communities of practice or through alignment with communities of practice within *or beyond* the congregation, congregational leaders and pastors are called to broker the relationship between communities of practice (confession of love) and confession of faith. Acting as bridge, brokers provide access to opportunities for a wider fellowship among the whole congregation, aligning the energies and momentum of the boundless conversations into a common vision for the future. Brokers encourage newcomers and established members to attend not only to local congregational mission, but also to broader ecumenical connections, conferences, denominational workshops, and events that provide encounters with the church at large—participating in these endeavors is itself a deep commitment to faithfulness. Providing members and newcomers alike with connections to the church at large paradoxically risks losing those members' energies or dedication to local concerns as new relationships and connections are made on a broader level. Yet it is through such a death that a new life is created, and through such a scattering that a new community is gathered.

Finally, newcomers are vital participants in developing new memories that become a present confession of faith. Through their provocative questions and acute observations, newcomers provoke a new articulation of the community's memory and graft to it their own storied past. Every newcomer has a history of participation or nonparticipation in other congregations (or other communities of practice outside congregations). Welcoming newcomers through legitimate peripheral participation ensures a place and space for their meanings, histories, and memories of other experiences from the broader communities of memory to be expressed. By creating this place and space in newcomer communities of practice, new meanings are created and in turn dispersed throughout the local congregation and beyond. Those newcomers who have relatively little or no background with the church are the cruciform witness to memory of the past. Their living questions rooted in the context of the world God loves juxtapose the present with the past. Without the witness of newcomers, the *ecclesia crucis* has no witness, for without the generational encounter, there is no ongoing story. Thus, the alignment of the present with the past within the church is cruciform—dying when it is static, only to rise to new life within a dynamic relationship with the world—existing only to be communicable in relation to the world.

CONFESSION OF HOPE

Unlike the memories of faithfulness, which are seen visibly affecting the identity of the communities of practice, the images of hope are glimpsed within communities of practice and often remain elusive and unformed. The images of hope still inform identity, but these formations are marks of promise etched upon a community's memory—promises to be lived into on the way. To confess hope for the future is to let the reality of the present and the past speak for itself, and from that reality to imagine the future. An image of hope provides opportunities for the communities of practice to reflect on their present-day relationship to the local church and imagine their role, as well as that of the individual members who constitute the community, in the church of the future and, more importantly, in courageous movement into the world.

Marked by the baptismal promise of dying and rising, hopeful congregations look at, rather than beyond, the suffering of the world. While this may seem like an odd understanding of hope, it is the radical eschatological image held by Martin Luther. Luther once allegedly quipped, "If I knew the world would end tomorrow, I'd plant a tree today."[2] Inspired by Luther, Douglas John Hall notes, "Faith is not sight, and hope is not arrival at the condition hoped for."[3] Hope remains in the future. It is elusive and just out of our grasp. At the same time, hope is embodied in a promise that marks the *ecclesia crucis* for daily dying and rising. Thus, hopeful congregations exist in the imagination of the *ecclesia crucis* while simultaneously being experienced in very decisive ways already.

The congregation of hope rests on the distinction between the theologian of glory and the theologian of the cross. The theologian of the cross insists on seeing the world as it is in all the despair and suffering of human sinfulness.[4] The theologian of glory is a theologian who hopes in life beyond this world. The glory story looks for God apart from the evil and suffering of the world. The cross story sees God in suffering and the cross. Hope is not platitudes and superficial optimism. Again, "faith is not sight and hope is not arrival at the condition hoped for."[5] Hope is visible in the world in a life lived under the cross. "The logic of the cross wants to keep us focused on the cross, which is not only Jesus' cross but the cross of the suffering creation that Jesus represents before God and on our behalf," Hall writes.[6] And for Luther, "The cross alone is our theology."[7]

Congregations live with hope, daily dying and rising with the continuity and displacement, reproduction and transformation that inherently take place in incarnate and human communities of practice. This hope recognizes the entropic forces that surround our local congregations, death and despair that are present in every life and every community on the earth. With their face set to the death of the cross, congregations rise with eyes set toward the future, imagining new possibilities for identity and belonging.

Hope is elusive. In this incompleteness, hope reminds the community of practice that knowledge is partial. The competence and participation of every person new and established is needed. Recognizing the incompetence and partiality of all is indicative of practicing disestablishment that leads to engagement. Established members within a congregation are always strangers, newcomers within evangelical worship.[8] Established members are strangers, welcomed over and over, again and again—daily—to the central practice of word and sacrament and the mutual conversation and consolation of the sisters and brothers. As they are shaped by these practices of daily dying and rising, Christ confronts them with truth, reminds them of their dependence upon God, and grants grace for the courage to become disciples—again.

Practicing the way of the cross, daily dying and rising, communities of practice imagine witness and service beyond their boundaries. Practicing the way of the cross, communities of practice confess hope bearing witness to the One who is Other. And this Other teaches us, through a cruciform catechesis, how to welcome others, to learn from others, and to be with others.[9] Hall notes, "The bearing or stance appropriate to the church is not that of a community that has arrived but of one that is under way (*communio viatorum*)—that is, a community of hope."[10] These hopeful congregations are under way, they are under the way of the cross, they are dying and rising as incarnate communities along the way of the incarnate God, who bids us to take up our cross and follow.

Congregations of hope are realized through the newcomers who come and "be-come" participants within communities of practice. Without newcomers, communities die; they turn in on themselves and away from the Other, the stranger, and the world God loves. At the same time, these newcomer strangers lurk threateningly, representing by their presence a hope for a new community that requires a death of the old. Yet, through the means of grace, communities of practice are shaped to die, so there is no fear in radically orienting to these newcomers and the world from which they come. Welcoming the Other and the stranger molds and shapes who we are and who we are to become. This dying and rising represents a radical reorientation to the world God loves.

PRACTICING DISESTABLISHMENT: CONFESSION OF FAITH, HOPE, AND LOVE

Our imaginations of who we are as the church in the future are shaped through encounters with newcomers. Through these encounters with newcomers, the *ecclesia crucis* becomes what we least expect it to be: a paradoxical community of memory, practice, and hope—broken yet holy, impure yet pure, temporary yet permanent, dying yet rising. Together, these three approaches—memory, practice, and hope—carry out the Deuteronomic injunction (Deut. 6:4-9) to pass on the central practices, the stories, and the cruciform hope that shapes the identity of disciples and the church from generation to generation. By attending to these three modes of belonging and clarifying their abilities and functions, congregations can design learning communities and be more effective at welcoming newcomers.

The gift of faith is an experience of God's promising presence as divine within the reality of the human condition. This experience of God as divine and human cultivates trust among humans, not through compulsion, but through a relationship in which Jesus Christ in the fullness of humanity seeks joy *and* sorrow, gladness *and* grief. Newcomers desire a relationship with Jesus Christ that is not static but fluid and dynamic, involving deep faith and honest doubt. Newcomers bring their questions, eager to receive faith as an experience of meaning in relationship with God and humanity and to explore the community's local and transcendent memory. A newcomer's questioning presence will offer hybridity and challenge the presumptive static identity of oldcomers. Newcomer questions will disarticulate oldcomer ways of knowing. Disestablishment is welcoming disarticulations within the *ecclesia crucis*. Oldcomers cannot respond defensively. Entertaining challenging questions means holding the tension between "my people" and "not my people." God's foolish, radical, inclusive love for the world demands that oldcomers linger in their own identity as "not my people." A newcomer's disarticulation is God's call to figure out our Christian identity in relation to one another at the boundary of the *simuls* (question) and *solas* (promise), the church and the world.

Being honest about the data of despair and suffering present in our lives and in the world, newcomers and oldcomers together live in the hope of the resurrection by looking toward the future with full regard for the world in which they are situated. To look at the suffering in the world is possible only with the faith and the courage given by God's grace. Hope-filled courage comes from faith and the promises contained within the means of grace (word, sacrament, and the Christian community). When the Holy Spirit gathers people together, promises are declared. The promise that oldcomers extend to newcomers is the promise of presence: "When you arrive, whenever you arrive, we are here." The congregation, gathered by the Holy Spirit to be disciples participating in Christian practices, is a promise announcing to the newcomer, "If you show up, we will be here, practicing faithfulness." Simultaneously, in questioning the promise, newcomers announce that the world is present within the congregation, and this in turn brings new life.

A confession of hope honest about suffering and pain engenders empathy and identification with the suffering that courageously calls upon *sola fides* (faith alone) to bear witness to the one who promises to be in relationship with us and yet appears in places and people where we least expect to see the Holy Triune's presence—in the newcomer. Love is doubt-filled, courageous living not for one's self but for the sake of one's neighbor. Congregations practice love through an orientation to the cross upon which God's *agape* (suffering love) is revealed. Here at the foot of the incarnate presence of the Crucified, whose spirit cried out in abandonment, the human spirit also cries, "Why?" Love becomes tangible as newcomers appear at the threshold of congregations, weary, broken, and worn, searching for meaning, purpose, identity, and new life. Love is the compulsion to welcome these newcomers, eager to hear their questions and to steward God's promises for them and not only for ourselves. This love transforms the congregation's orientation toward God and to the world.

"We have a way." This is the response that congregations within the Evangelical Lutheran Church in America (ELCA) practicing the catechumenate give to newcomers and inquirers of the faith.

- We have a way to welcome you.
- We have a way to encourage and explore your questions about Jesus and the Christian faith.
- We have a way to facilitate your participation and belonging in this church and your baptismal vocation in the world.

In having a way for newcomers, we have a way forward for the whole church. The future of the church demands that we attend to the questions of liminals and nones.

To welcome newcomers, I have proposed a cruciform catechesis, a type of learning that arises from newcomers and established members participating together in Christian discipleship practices over time. This way of learning together welcomes newcomers and oldcomers in inclusive ways, encouraging exploration around the person of Jesus Christ and the resources of faith, and facilitating newcomer participation personally in the particular local practices lived out in congregations. Only *as* disciples can we learn what it means to *be* disciples of the cross. To learn to be a disciple is to participate in the church's commitment to figuring out what faithfulness looks like in every era by learning the practices and stories of Jesus and the witness of the first followers of Jesus. A cruciform catechesis is an ecclesiological discipleship-making process that takes the conditions and reality of the world today seriously, insisting that newcomers are indispensable participants of the *ecclesia crucis*.

The *ecclesia crucis* cannot seek permanence with oldcomers as the solid foundation, but must seek fluidity and movement with newcomers and oldcomers participating in life together under the cross. Thus, the life of the church depends upon a newcomer's presence within the body of Christ. Newcomers may be an unsettling presence, but they are saving the church. A cruciform catechesis gives rise to the *ecclesia crucis*, and the *ecclesia crucis* shapes a cruciform catechesis. Newcomers and oldcomers recognize their discipleship on the way as shaped by their mutual commitment to the task of figuring it out. At the same time, the *ecclesia crucis* becomes the locus—the space—in which communities of practice arise by designing opportunities for learning through a cruciform catechesis. In theory, this ministry of welcoming newcomers attempts to balance the movement of a disestablished community within congregations while offering a clear and intentionally designed process to facilitate newcomer welcome, learning, and participation.

To be a Christian church is to practice being a people under the cross, practicing a confession of faith, hope, and love, welcoming newcomers into discipleship practices where faith meets doubt, hope meets despair, and love meets the suffering world. In this very process of welcoming newcomers, God saves the church, moving the church into relationship with the world. Like building sand castles, this is a pretty foolish way of being church. I have written this book so the church can remember how to be church, marked by faith, hope, and love. Welcome the very next person who arrives at the threshold of your congregation in this way. Invite him or her along on your way to the cross. Come and see! Come participate! Come learn! Come and be gathered to confess faith and hope. Come and be sent to love the suffering world! *Soli Deo Gloria.*

Notes

1. Etienne Wenger, *Communities of Practice: Learning, Meaning, and Identity*, Learning in Doing: Social Cognitive, and Computational Perspectives, ed. John Seely Brown (Cambridge: Cambridge University Press, 1998), 277.

2. Posthumously attributed to Luther, although he probably never said it.

3. Douglas John Hall, *The Cross in Our Context: Jesus and the Suffering World* (Minneapolis: Fortress Press, 2003), 195.

4. Timothy F. Lull, ed. *Martin Luther's Basic Theological Writings* (Minneapolis: Fortress Press, 1989), 31.

5. Hall, *The Cross in Our Context*, 216.

6. Ibid.

7. Gerhard O. Forde, *On Being a Theologian of the Cross: Reflections on Luther's Heidelberg Disputation, 1518* (Grand Rapids: Eerdmans, 1997), 3. [Original quote: Martin Luther, *Operationes in Luther's Commentary on the First Twenty-two Psalms,* trans. John Nicholas Lenker (Sunbury, PA: Lutherans in All Lands Co., 1903), 1:289.]

8. Gordon W. Lathrop, *Holy Things: A Liturgical Theology* (Minneapolis: Fortress Press, 1993), 119.

9. Hall, *The Cross in Our Context*, 195.

10. Ibid.

Appendix: Research Methodology

This research was based on the following descriptive question:[1]

What role does the adult catechumenate play in the faith formation of newcomers and established members, i.e.:

- How does the catechumenate form and affect the faith and spiritual practices of new members (both newly baptized and transfers)?
- Does the catechumenate form and affect the faith and spiritual practices of sponsors?

Within this research question, I was interested in the following subareas:

1. *Does the catechumenate help them learn more about the Lutheran/ Christian tradition?* Have you learned more about your Lutheran identity? What does it mean to be a Christian? Did the catechumenate process significantly shape your identity as a Christian or as a Lutheran?

2. *Does it connect with their personal faith journey and encourage them to participate in spiritual practices at home and in the church?* Do you feel like this congregation has connected with where you are at this point on your journey of faith? Has the catechumenate process connected with your personal faith journey? Has the catechumenate process taught you any spiritual practices?

3. *Does the catechumenate enhance their participation in church?* How often do you attend worship? Do you participate in any church activities? Has the catechumenate significantly changed your participation habits?

4. *Does it increase their sense of belonging?* Have you made significant connections with others in this congregation? How many of your total friends are in this congregation? Has the catechumenate significantly changed your sense of belonging?

5. *Does it increase their comfort with evangelism and/or encourage participation in social outreach?* How comfortable are you talking about your faith with others? Are you more involved in community service, social service, and advocacy?

RESEARCH DESIGN

The criterion I used to define my sample was the congregation's willingness to self-identify as engaging in catechumenal ministry. My sample was not random, and the congregation's self-identification was of interest to my research. There is no listing of all the Evangelical Lutheran Church in America (ELCA) congregations that participate in the catechumenate.[2] In the fall of 2004, I attended an ELCA Catechumenate Task Force, meeting with fifteen pastors and lay people interested in the catechumenate. Together, these individuals listed eighteen ELCA congregations that are practicing the catechumenate. When I returned home, an Internet search led to the discovery of fifteen additional catechumenate congregations in the ELCA.

I do not believe there is a typical case of the practice of the catechumenate. In fact, among the congregations I have identified as practicing the catechumenate, there is a wide diversity of commitment to the practice. Additionally, the practice seems to be functioning better at some congregations than at others. One or two of these congregations could be considered a "best-practices congregation." Therefore, the selection of my final sample of eight congregations looked toward maximizing variation among the churches, following the methodological principle "to integrate only a few cases, but those which are as different as possible to disclose the range of variation and differentiation in the field."[3] (See Table 1.)

TABLE 1: CONGREGATIONS STUDIED

Code	Year Established	Staff	Population/ Location	Average Worship	Lay Catechists	Years of Catechumenate	Catechumenate Initiated by
A	1765	1 pastor	11,600/ bourough, Mid-Atlantic	96	1	7	Lay catechist
B	1846	1 pastor	26,263/small city, Mid-Atlantic	72	1	7	Pastor
C	1852	1 pastor	30,700/small city, Mid-Atlantic	190	1	6	Pastor
D	1915	2 pastors	573,900/large city, Northwest	315	4 or 5	11	Congregation
E	1920	1 pastor	11,600/borough, Mid-Atlantic	80	1	4	Pastor
F	1922	Pastor, AIM[a]	187,300/medium city, South	238	1	10b	Lay catechist
G	1940	1 pastor	205,648/medium city, South	77	0	4	Pastor
H	1959	1 pastor	55,351/small city, Mid-Atlantic	140	1	3	Pastor

Among the eight congregations I studied, I conducted the following qualitative research methods (adapting the research design in cases where the practice of the catechumenate in a congregation did not match this structure perfectly):

- **Semistructured interview** with church leaders (pastors, associates) and catechumenate leaders (catechists).
- **Two focus groups** with parishioners who had joined the church in the preceding five years. One group included only those who had participated in the catechumenate process, and another consisted of those who had not.
- **One focus group** with parishioners who had participated in the catechumenate process as sponsors within the preceding five years.
- **Observation** of relevant worship services and programs (classes, small groups, Bible studies, etc.) over a three-day period. In cases where I could participate in the rites of the catechumenate or catechumenate Bible study, I was involved in participant observation. I also used videography and photography to illustrate the rites of the catechumenate process and to capture location information.
- **Phone interviews** with one key informant in five additional catechumenate congregations during the summer of 2005. The aim of these conversations was to listen for the successes and failures of the catechumenate process in congregations other than the eight I visited.

I kept detailed notes, given my own participation in this process, to triangulate my data. I attempted to engage in thematic coding of the data I received. Thematic coding is a process "in which the groups that are studied are derived from the research question and thus defined a priori."[4] Data in thematic coding are collected with the goal of comparing analysis. The procedure for thematic coding is as follows:

1. Write a short description of the case (checked, rechecked, and modified).
2. In a deepened analysis of the case, develop a system of categories through open and selective coding.
3. Cross-check the cases.
4. Develop thematic structure.

This process is designed to result in "a case-oriented display of the way the case specifically deals with the issue of the study, including constant topics which can be found in the viewpoints across different domains."[5] I also aimed to triangulate the data I collected with a review of current research on the assimilation of newcomers within congregations.

Notes

1. I chose a descriptive research question because I was interested in how each congregation and each individual understood the catechumenate. I also asked generative questions because I did not have a given hypothesis for how these questions would be answered in the various congregations I studied. Uwe Flick, *An Introduction to Qualitative Research*, 2nd ed. (London: SAGE, 2002), 50.

2. In 1994, under the leadership of the Associate Director of Worship for the ELCA, a catechumenate question was placed on the ELCA parochial report: "Do you practice the catechumenate in your congregation?" Unfortunately, as information was being collected, follow-up calls revealed that the question was vastly misunderstood. Many pastors filling out the report thought the question was in reference to confirmation and catechesis, not the process of the catechumenate.

3. Flick, *An Introduction to Qualitative Research*, 68.

4. Ibid., 185.

5. Ibid., 188.

Bibliography

Ammerman, Nancy Tatom. *Congregation and Community.* New Brunswick: Rutgers University Press, 1997.

———. *Pillars of Faith: American Congregations and Their Partners.* Berkeley: University of California Press, 2005.

Bass, Diana Butler. *Christianity for the Rest of Us: How the Neighborhood Church Is Transforming the Faith.* San Francisco: HarperSanFrancisco, 2006.

———. *The Practicing Congregation: Imagining a New Old Church.* Herndon, VA: Alban Institute, 2004.

Bass, Dorothy C., ed. *Practicing Our Faith: A Way of Life for a Searching People.* Practices of Faith Series, edited by Dorothy C. Bass. San Francisco: Jossey-Bass, 1997.

Bass, Dorothy, and Craig Dykstra. "Christian Practices and Congregational Education in Faith." In *Churches: The Local Church and the Structures of Change.* Edited by Michael Warren. Portland, OR: Pastoral Press of Oregon Catholic Press, 2000.

Becker, Ernest. *The Denial of Death.* New York: Free Press, 1973.

Benedict, Daniel. *Come to the Waters: Baptism and Our Ministry of Welcoming Seekers and Making Disciples.* Nashville: Discipleship Resources, 1996.

Bliese, Richard H., and Craig Van Gelder, eds. *The Evangelizing Church: A Lutheran Contribution.* Minneapolis: Augsburg Fortress, 2005.

Boys, Mary C. *Education in Faith: Maps and Visions.* Lima, OH: Academic Renewal, 1989.

Burns, John. "Building Sand Castles: Tips." *essortment,* http://il.essortment.com/buildsandcastl_rxcq.htm.

Bushkofsky, Dennis. "Welcome to Christ: Preparing Adults for Baptism and Discipleship." Chicago: Division for Congregational Ministries, Evangelical Lutheran Church in America, 1998.

———. *What Do You Seek? Welcoming the Adult Inquirer.* Minneapolis: Augsburg Fortress, 2000.

Carter, Craig A. *Rethinking Christ and Culture.* Grand Rapids: Brazos, 2006.

Cruchley-Jones, Peter. "Entering Exile: Can There Be a Missiology for 'Not My People'?" In *A Scandalous Prophet: The Way of Mission after Newbigin.* Edited by Thomas F. Foust, George R. Hunsburger, J. Andrew Kirk, and Werner Ustorf, 23–36. Grand Rapids: Eerdmans, 2002.

Day, Juliette. *Baptism in Early Byzantine Palestine, 325–451.* Joint Liturgical Studies. Cambridge: Cambridge Books, 1999.

Dykstra, Craig. *Growing in the Life of Faith: Education and Christian Practices.* 2nd ed. Louisville: Westminster John Knox, 2005.

Episcopal Office of Evangelism Ministries. *The Catechumenal Process: Adult Initiation and Formation for Christian Life and Ministry.* New York: Church Hymnal Corporation, 1990.

Evangelical Lutheran Church in America (ELCA). *Evangelical Lutheran Worship.* Minneapolis: Augsburg Fortress, 2006.

———. *The Use of the Means of Grace: A Statement on the Practice of Word and Sacrament.* Minneapolis: ELCA, 1997.

Everist, Norma Cook. *The Church as Learning Community: A Comprehensive Guide to Christian Education.* Nashville: Abingdon, 2002.

Forde, Gerhard O. *On Being a Theologian of the Cross: Reflections on Luther's Heidelberg Disputation, 1518.* Grand Rapids: Eerdmans, 1997.

Frend, W. H. C. *The Rise of Christianity.* Philadelphia: Fortress Press, 1984.

Gassmann, Gunther, and Scott Hendrix. *Fortress Introduction to the Lutheran Confessions.* Minneapolis: Fortress Press, 1999.

Go Make Disciples: An Invitation to Baptismal Living. Minneapolis: Augsburg Fortress, 2012.

Gowan, Donald E. "Amos." In *The New Interpreter's Bible.* Edited by Leander Keck. Nashville: Abingdon, 1996.

Gramsci, Antonio. "Hegemony, Intellectuals, and the State." In *Cultural Theory and Popular Culture: A Reader.* Edited by John Storey. Harlow: Pearson Education, 2006.

Grant, George. *Technology and Justice.* Toronto: Anansi, 1969.

Grime, Paul, Donald W. Johnson, Marcus J. Miller, Gail Ramshaw, Martin A. Seltz, Robert Buckley Farlee, and May L. Schwarz. *Welcome to Christ: Lutheran Rites for the Catechumenate.* Edited by Paul Nelson, Frank Stoldt, Scott Weidler, and Lani Willis. Minneapolis: Augsburg Fortress, 1997.

Groome, Thomas H., and Harold D. Horell, eds. *Horizons and Hopes: The Future of Religious Education.* New York: Paulist, 2003.

Hall, Douglas John. *Bound and Free: A Theologian's Journey.* Minneapolis: Fortress Press, 2005.

———. *Confessing the Faith: Christian Theology in a North American Context.* Minneapolis: Fortress Press, 1996.

———. *The Cross in Our Context: Jesus and the Suffering World.* Minneapolis: Fortress Press, 2003.

———. *The End of Christendom and the Future of Christianity.* Christian Mission and Modern Culture, edited by Alan Neely, H. Wayne Pipkin, and Wilbert R. Shenk. Valley Forge, PA: Trinity Press International, 1997.

———. *Lighten Our Darkness: Toward an Indigenous Theology of the Cross.* Philadelphia: Westminster, 1976.

———. "The Theology of the Cross: A Usable Past." Evangelical Lutheran Church in America, http://www.elca.org/~/media/Files/ Growing%20in%20Faith/Vocation/Word%20and%20Service%20Ministry/ TheTheologyoftheCross_pdf.ashx.

———. "Theology of the Cross: Challenge and Opportunity for the Post-Christendom Church." In *Cross Examinations: Readings on the Meaning of the Cross Today.* Edited by Marit Trelstad, 252–58. Minneapolis: Fortress Press, 2006.

———. *Thinking the Faith: Christian Theology in a North American Context.* Vol. 1. Minneapolis: Fortress Press, 1991.

———. *Why Christian?* Minneapolis: Augsburg Fortress, 1998.

Hendrix, Scott H. *Recultivating the Vineyard: The Reformation Agendas of Christianization.* Louisville, KY: Westminster John Knox, 2004.

Hütter, Reinhard. *Suffering Divine Things: Theology as Church Practice.* Translated by Doug Stott. Grand Rapids: Eerdmans, 2000.

Hymans, Diane J. "Education and Evangelism: Is the Connection Essential?" In *Christian Education as Evangelism.* Edited by Norma Cook Everist. Minneapolis: Fortress Press, 2007.

International Commission on English in the Liturgy. *The Rites of the Catholic Church.* New York: Pueblo, 1976.

Johnson, Maxwell E. *The Rites of Christian Initiation: Their Evolution and Interpretation.* Revised and expanded ed. Collegeville, MN: Liturgical, 2007.

Kaspersen, Lars Bo. *Anthony Giddens: An Introduction to a Social Theorist.* Translated by Steven Sampson. Malden, MA: Blackwell, 2000.

Kolb, Robert, and Timothy J. Wengert, eds. *The Book of Concord: The Confessions of the Evangelical Lutheran Church.* Minneapolis: Fortress Press, 2000.

Lathrop, Gordon W. *Holy Things: A Liturgical Theology.* Minneapolis: Fortress Press, 1993.

Lathrop, Gordon W., and Timothy J. Wengert. *Christian Assembly: Marks of the Church in a Pluralistic Age.* Minneapolis: Fortress Press, 2004.

Lave, Jean, and Etienne Wenger. *Situated Learning: Legitimate Peripheral Participation.* Learning in Doing: Social, Cognitive, and Computational Perspectives, edited by John Seely Brown. Cambridge: Cambridge University Press, 1991.

Lawless, Chuck. *Membership Matters: Insights from Effective Churches on New Member Classes and Assimilation.* Grand Rapids, MI: Zondervan, 2005.

———. *Living Witnesses: The Adult Catechumenate: A Manual for the Catechumenal Process.* Manitoba: n.p., 1994.

Lull, Timothy F., ed. *Martin Luther's Basic Theological Writings.* Minneapolis: Fortress Press, 1989.

Luther, Martin. "The Large Catechism." In Kolb and Wengert, *The Book of Concord: The Confessions of the Evangelical Lutheran Church.*

———. *Lectures on Romans, Glosses and Scholia.* Vol. 25 of *Luther's Works.* Translated by Jacob A. Preus. Edited by Jaroslav Pelikan and Helmut T. Lehmann. St. Louis: Concordia Publishing House, 1972.

———. *Selected Psalms III.* Vol. 14 of *Luther's Works.* Translated by Jaroslav Pelikan. Edited by Jaroslav Pelikan. St. Louis: Concordia Publishing House, 1958.

MacIntyre, Alasdair C. *After Virtue: A Study in Moral Theology.* Notre Dame, IN: University of Notre Dame Press, 1984.

Marty, Martin E. "Articles of War, Articles of Peace: Christianity and Culture." In *Christ and Culture in Dialogue: Constructive Themes and Practical Applications.* Edited by Angus J. L. Menuge. St. Louis: Concordia Academic, 1999.

McGinn, Bernard. *The Foundations of Mysticism: Origins to the Fifth Century.* Vol. 1, *The Presence of God: A History of Western Mysticism.* New York: Crossroad, 1994.

McIntosh, Gary, and Glen Martin. *Finding Them, Keeping Them: Effective Strategies for Evangelism and Assimilation in the Local Church.* Nashville: Broadman & Holman, 1992.

Mercer, Joyce. *Welcoming Children: A Practical Theology of Childhood.* St. Louis: Chalice, 2005.

Morris, Thomas H. *The RCIA: Transforming the Church: A Resource for Pastoral Implementation.* Revised and updated ed. New York: Paulist, 1997.

Nessan, Craig L. "After the Death of Evangelism: The Resurrection of an Evangelizing Church." In *The Evangelizing Church: A Lutheran Contribution.*

Edited by Richard H. Bliese and Craig Van Gelder. Minneapolis: Augsburg Fortress, 2005.

Niebuhr, H. Richard. *Christ and Culture.* San Francisco: HarperSanFrancisco, 2001.

Nussbaum, Martha C. *Sex and Social Justice.* New York: Oxford University Press, 1999.

Olson, Daniel V. A. "Learning from Lyle Schaller: Social Aspects of Congregations." *Christian Century,* January 27, 1993, 83–84.

Osmer, Richard R. *Confirmation: Presbyterian Practices in Ecumenical Perspective.* Louisville, KY: Geneva, 1996.

———. *Practical Theology: An Introduction.* Grand Rapids: Eerdmans, 2008.

———. *The Teaching Ministry of Congregations.* Louisville, KY: Westminster/John Knox, 2005.

Osmer, Richard R., and Friedrich Schweitzer. *Religious Education between Modernization and Globalization.* Studies in Practical Theology, edited by James W. Fowler, Don S. Browning, Friedrich Schweitzer, and Johannes A. van der Ven. Grand Rapids: Eerdmans, 2003.

Oswald, Roy M. *New Beginnings: A Pastorate Start Up Workbook.* [Washington, DC]: Alban Institute, 1989.

Oswald, Roy M., and Speed B. Leas. *The Inviting Church: A Study of New Member Assimilation.* Washington, DC: Alban Institute, 1987.

Piro, Beverly. *Welcome to Christ: Sponsors Guide.* Edited by Robert Buckley Farlee and Becky Lowe. Minneapolis: Augsburg Fortress, 2002.

Putnam, Robert, and David Campbell. *American Grace: How Religion Unites and Divides Us.* New York: Simon and Schuster, 2010.

Rajashekar, J. Paul. "Navigating Difficult Questions." In *The Evangelizing Church: A Lutheran Contribution.* Edited by Richard H. Bliese and Craig Van Gelder. Minneapolis: Augsburg Fortress, 2005.

Randall, Dennis. "Stupendous Sandcastles: An Imagination Station Activity." *Family Education* (Pearson Education), http://fun.familyeducation.com/summer/outdoor-games/35066.html.

Rendtorff, Rolf. *The Covenant Formula: An Exegetical and Theological Investigation.* Translated by Margaret Kohl. Edited by David J. Reimer. Old Testament Studies. Edinburgh: T & T Clark, 1998.

Roof, Wade Clark, and William McKinney. *American Mainline Religion: Its Changing Shape and Future.* 4th ed. New Brunswick, NJ: Rutgers University Press, 1987.

Schaller, Lyle E. *Assimilating New Members.* Creative Leadership Series, edited by Lyle E. Schaller. Nashville: Abingdon, 1978.

Senn, Frank C. *Christian Liturgy: Catholic and Evangelical.* Minneapolis: Fortress Press, 1997.

Solberg, Mary M. "All That Matters: What an Epistemology of the Cross Is Good For." In *Cross Examinations: Readings on the Meaning of the Cross Today.* Edited by Marit Trelstad, 139–53. Minneapolis: Fortress Press, 2006.

Storey, John. *Cultural Theory and Popular Culture: An Introduction.* 4th ed. Athens: University of Georgia Press, 2006.

Tanner, Kathryn. *Theories of Culture: A New Agenda for Theology.* Guides to Theological Inquiry. Minneapolis: Fortress Press, 1997.

Tillich, Paul. *Systematic Theology.* Vol. 1. Chicago: University of Chicago Press, 1951.

Torvend, Samuel, and Lani Willis, eds. *Welcome to Christ: A Lutheran Catechetical Guide.* Minneapolis: Augsburg Fortress, 1997.

———. *Welcome to Christ: A Lutheran Introduction to the Catechumenate.* Minneapolis: Augsburg Fortress, 1997.

Ward, Karen. *Welcome to Christ: Preparing Adults for Baptism and Discipleship.* Chicago: Division for Congregational Ministries, Evangelical Lutheran Church in America, 1998. Video.

Wenger, Etienne. *Communities of Practice: Learning, Meaning, and Identity.* Learning in Doing: Social, Cognitive, and Computational Perspectives, edited by John Seely Brown. Cambridge: Cambridge University Press, 1998.

Wenger, Etienne, Richard McDermott, and William M Snyder. *Cultivating Communities of Practice: A Guide to Managing Knowledge.* Boston: Harvard Business School Press, 2002.

Index